Conveyancing Fees and Duties

Thirty Third Edition

compiled by Russell Hewitson LLB Solicitor of the School of Law, Northumbria University

Tottel Publishing Ltd, Maxwelton House, 41-43 Boltro Road, Haywards Heath, West Sussex, RH16 1BJ

© Tottel Publishing Ltd 2009

All rights reserved. No part of this publication may be reproduced in any material form (including photocopying or storing it in any medium by electronic means and whether or not transiently or incidentally to some other use of this publication) without the written permission of the copyright owner except in accordance with the provisions of the Copyright, Designs and Patents Act 1988 or under the terms of a licence issued by the Copyright Licensing Agency Ltd, Saffron House, 6-10 Kirby Street, London, England EC1N 8TS. Applications for the copyright owner's written permission to reproduce any part of this publication should be addressed to the publisher.

Warning: The doing of an unauthorised act in relation to a copyright work may result in both a civil claim for damages and criminal prosecution.

Crown copyright material is reproduced with the permission of the Controller of HMSO and the Queen's Printer for Scotland. Any European material in this work which has been reproduced from EUR-lex, the official European Communities legislation website, is European Communities copyright.

A CIP Catalogue record for this book is available from the British Library.

ISBN-978 1 84766 302 3

Typeset by Letterpart Ltd, Reigate, Surrey

Printed in Great Britain by Athenaeum, Gateshead, Tyne and Wear

CONTENTS

1. Stamp Duty Land Tax 5
   1.1 Introduction 5
   1.2 HM Revenue & Customs publications 5
   1.3 General information 12
   1.4 "Chargeable consideration" 14
   1.5 "Disadvantaged Area Relief" and other reliefs and exemptions 15
   1.6 Rates of SDLT on the "chargeable consideration" 16
   1.7 SDLT on the grant of a lease 17
2. Land Registry 19
   2.1 Land Registry Offices 19
   2.2 Land Registry "Practice Guides" 21
   2.3 Application and Search Forms 23
   2.4 Land Registry Fees 26
   2.5 Land Charges Department 35
3. Local land charges – searches and enquiries (including a list of local authorities) 37
4. Drainage and Water searches 42
5. Commons Registration search 44
6. Environmental searches and reports 44
7. Coal mining searches and reports 44
8. Tin and copper mining searches in parts of South West England 45
9. China Clay searches 46
10. Radon searches 47
11. Cheshire brine subsidence searches 47
12. Companies House 48
13. Gypsum mining 51
14. Land Registry Direct 51
15. The National Land Information Service ("NLIS") 52
16. Information available from "English Heritage" 53
17. London underground searches 54
18. Ordnance Survey information 54
19. Chancel repair 54
20. Rates of interest under s 32 Land Compensation Act 1961 55
21. Law Society interest rates 56
22. Other telephone numbers 57

STAMP DUTY LAND TAX ("SDLT")

This publication contains sources of information for "residential" conveyancing transactions in England and Wales. It is intended as a guide, so that specialist information and advice about Stamp Duty Land Tax (and all other tax implications) should always be obtained. That is particularly important where the transaction is the grant of a new lease or a "partnership", "commercial" or unusual "residential" conveyancing transaction.

1. STAMP DUTY LAND TAX ("SDLT")

1.1 INTRODUCTION

The primary legislation is contained in sections 42 to 124 and Schedules 3 to 19 to the Finance Act 2003 and sections 296 to 305 and Schedules 38 to 41 to the Finance Act 2004.

Further information can be found at www.hmrc.gov.uk/so/sdlt.

1.2 HM REVENUE & CUSTOMS PUBLICATIONS

HMRC publishes Guidance Notes (SDLT6) which are available at www.hmrc.gov.uk/sdlt6/index.htm. These are updated regularly and assist in completing the prescribed forms of land transaction return and interpreting the legislation.

The following is a list of HMRC's *SDLT Practitioners' News* (formerly *SDLT Practitioners' Newsletters* Issues 1 to 6 and the contents of each), as published since May 2004. Please check the HMRC website for subsequent updates.

Title and subjects covered	Date of issue
Practitioners' Newsletters:	
Issue 1:	
Common errors on completing SDLT1 returns	May 2004
Issue 2:	July 2004
Penalties for late Land Transaction returns – a reminder	
Using the National Land & Property Gazetteer – Unique Property Reference Number (NLPG UPRN)	
When an SDLT1 should be submitted	
When plans need to be submitted with an SDLT1	
How to complete boxes 9 & 10 on the SDLT1 form	
Payment of SDLT through BACS Direct Credit	
DX exchange numbers and the use of Hays-DX courier envelopes	
Corrections to the previous (1st) issue of the Practitioners' Newsletter	
Appendix – Common queries regarding leases	
Issue 3:	September 2004
SDLT1-errors and processing issues	
SDLT CD-Rom	
SDLT8s: when they will be issued	
Multiple Acquisitions	
SDLT: calculating amount due	

STAMP DUTY LAND TAX ("SDLT")

    Advice on when you can use an SDLT60 instead of an SDLT1 to notify a transaction
    Complaints
    Supplementary forms: sending photocopies
    Using the same transaction number on every SDLT1 submitted
    Clarification to May's Practitioners' Newsletter
    Previous issues of the Practitioners' Newsletter

Issue 4:   December 2004
    New SDLT forms 8,9, 11 and 12
    SDLT CD-Rom
    SDLT pilot
    Which aspects of the SDLT process present the most difficulties?
    Stamp Taxes Enquiry Line and IR Orderline
    Use of DX numbers
    Relief claimed on "right to buy" transactions
    One cheque submitted covering multiple applications
    Disposal and charities relief
    Leases
    SDLT and "nil-rate band Discretionary trusts"
    Clarification to October's Practitioners' Newsletter
    Previous issues of the Practitioners' Newsletter
    Future SDLT guidance
    Updating our mailing list

Issue 5:   January 2005
    Special newsletter – information on the SDLT CD Rom

Issue 6:   February 2005
    SDLT 6 guidance and Stamp Taxes website inserts
    SDLT CD Rom
    Updated CD Rom help screen message in respect of Question 13 – "Linked Transactions"
    Which aspects of SDLT present the most difficulties
    Quoting the Unique Transaction Reference Number (UTRN)
    National Land & Property Gazetteer – Unique Property Reference Number (NLPG UPRN)
    New version of SDLT 4
    SDLT Compliance Regime
    SDLT payment issues
    Ordering SDLT forms
    Reversionary Leases
    Clarification to the flyer on new SDLT forms (8, 9, 11 and 12) issued with the previous Practitioners' Newsletter
    Previous issues of the Practitioners' Newsletter
    Updating our mailing list

Issue 7:   April 2005
    SDLT6 guidance insert
    Do you use SDLT forms supplied by Legal or Software Suppliers?
    Completion of the SDLT1: Tips for avoiding rejections
    Non-residential transactions
    SDLT forms

STAMP DUTY LAND TAX ("SDLT")

What do I do if my certificate is incorrect?
Help us to make sure your certificate and/or correspondence is delivered to you first time
Sending correspondence to our Rapid Data Capture Centre in Bootle
Sample SDLT forms available on our website
SDLT payment issues
Making SDLT payments by CHAPS
Partnerships under SDLT
Schedules for under/sub leases
SDLT and 'nil-rate band discretionary trusts'
Transfers of property subject to a debt, and variation of testamentary dispositions
SDLT12/12a: letter advising an underpayment has been made and the balance is required and / or a penalty imposed
SDLT CD Rom
Freedom of Information Act
References in Stamp Duty/SDLT leaflets to 0870 & 0845 numbers as being charged at 'local rates'
Stock Transfer forms

Issue 8:   June 2005
Clarification to the previous newsletter
SDLT1 completion & SDLT8 queries
SDLT1 Question 10
Completing Questions 52 & 54 on the SDLT1 return
Actions that prevent SDLT returns from being processed
Circumstances in which an SDLT8 letter will be issued
Completion of SDLT returns
SDLT2• SDLT 4
Making manual alterations on barcoded SDLT returns
Changing to barcoded forms
SDLT CD-Rom
Other SDLT issues
Disadvantaged Area Relief-Submission of non-residential SDLT returns
SDLT transactions that should be sent to the Stamp Taxes Complex Transactions Unit in Manchester
Stop Press
SDLT: The Budget 2005 proposals
Including the agent reference number on the SDLT5 certificate
Revised SDLT6 guidance notes
SDLT: Requests for payment in error
SDLT9 & 12: Letters received relating to refunds or overpayments for zero value
SDLT quick guides
Appendix
Previous issues of the Practitioners' Newsletter
Updating our mailing list

Issue 9:   September 2005
Important SDLT changes
New On-line completion and submission service (full On-line filing)

STAMP DUTY LAND TAX ("SDLT")

Interest charged on late or unpaid SDLT or penalties
SDLT – Changes to submission of Land Transaction Returns
Completion of SDLT returns
SDLT8 completion
Examination of SDLT8 errors
How to submit your SDLT returns
Other SDLT issues
SDLT Return – PS1/SDLT payslips – Wrong UTRN
New version of form SDLT60 (certification that no SDLT return is required for a land transaction)
SDLT Manual – Revised lease chapter
Clarification to the previous newsletter (Issue 8-June 2005)
Sending correspondence to our Rapid Data Capture Centre in Bootle
Who may act as a purchaser's 'agent'
Total consideration
Working together on SDLT
SDLT CD Rom Frequently Asked Questions
Ordering SDLT forms in January 2006
Appendix
Previous issues of the Practitioners' Newsletter

Issue 10:   February 2005
SDLT returns
Linking up a supplementary return with the main SDLT1 return
Completion of house numbers within addresses required on the SDLT1 return
SDLT5 issues
SDLT6 Guidance notes
New version of form SDLT60 (certification that no SDLT return is required for a land transaction)
DX addresses
Our new online product – Online Tax Return – Land Transaction
A new service availability page on the HMRC website
Online Tax Return – Land Transaction product issues
Limited Liability Partnerships registering to use the Online Tax Return – Land Transaction product
Electronic payment
2-d barcode issues
SDLT – Rejected black & white returns
Other SDLT & general issues
Clarification to the previous newsletter
Reorganisation of work within Stamp Taxes
SDLT penalties for the late submission of the SDLT1 return
Interest charged on late or unpaid SDLT or penalties
HMRC services for disabled customers
SDLT policy on compensation claims
Stamp Taxes: implications of Civil Partnerships Act 2004
16 day urgency service for purchasers in Scotland
What if I have paid too much SDLT?

8

STAMP DUTY LAND TAX ("SDLT")

    The main sources of SDLT guidance
    Power of Attorney
    Ordering SDLT returns online
    Stamp Taxes Internet site development update
    Navigation within our SDLT manual
    Appendix
    Previous issues of the Practitioners' Newsletter
    Updating our mailing list
    SDLT returns

Issue 11:   June 2006
    News
    Closure of London Stamp Office counter service
    Movement of Stamp Taxes operations from Worthing Stamp Office to Birmingham Stamp Office
    Future online versions of this newsletter
    SDLT Technical Newsletter
    SDLT Returns
    Including purchaser's & vendor's address details on the SDLT1
    Completing SDLT1 Returns – common errors
    'Missing' SDLT1s – fax process
    Awaiting a certificate for a transaction where a Supplementary SDLT Return has also been submitted
    Receipt of original documents enclosed with SDLT applications at our Processing Centre
    Stamp Taxes Online
    Computer Requirements
    Service availability
    Customer Feedback
    Other SDLT & general issues
    Revised online version of the SDLT6 guidance notes
    Grants and assignments of leases
    Self-certification using form SDLT60 – new versions of SDLT60 self-certification form & SDLT68 guidance
    SDLT appeal forms (SDLT46 & 47)
    Interest repayments
    SDLT Payments
    Form 64-8
    Stamp Taxes Calculator & SDLT on Lease Transactions Calculator
    Stamp Taxes & HMRC website
    Appendix
    Previous issues of the SDLT Practitioners' Newsletter

Issue 12:   August 2006
    Renaming of the SDLT Practitioners' Newsletter
    Interest repayments
    New Post Office charging criteria
    Receipt of original documents enclosed with SDLT applications at our Data Capture Centre
    SDLT Payments
    HMRC services for customers with special requirements
    Late filing penalties, Minimum information required on SDLT1 returns
    Feedback

STAMP DUTY LAND TAX ("SDLT")

Previous issues of the SDLT Practitioners' Newsletter

Issue 13: September 2006
Special issue on the introduction of the Electronic SDLT5 certificate
Previous issues of the SDLT Practitioners' Newsletter

Issue 14: November 2006
New guidance for online lease notification (19th October 06)
Multiple Linked Grants of Lease Guidance
Users of TPV internet filing software
Maintain agent details (1st November 06)
Validation change to 'Start date of lease' (April 07)
Upgrades to HMRC's web portal (June 07)
Future online enhancements (2007)

Issue 14 November 2006
Stamp Taxes Online: Further Enhancements
Previous issues of the SDLT Practitioners' Newsletter
Quick Links

Issue 15 November 2006
Automated Registration of Title to Land (ARTL) and the e-conveyancing project
Previous issues of the SDLT Practitioners' Newsletter
Quick Links

Issue 16 December 2006
Electronic SDLT5 certificate
Birmingham Stamp Office: change of address
Penalty letter responses
Why SDLT8 letters are issued
Ringing the changes for SDLT8s
Vendor's address (SDLT1, Questions 34 – 38)
Agent details (SDLT1, Questions 57-62)
The Welsh Language Act 1993
2-D bar-coded/CD-Rom notifications
New SDLT Form 46 – Appeal against a penalty determination
New rates of interest on stamp taxes paid late and overpaid
Feedback
Previous issues of the SDLT Practitioners' Newsletter
Quick Links

Issue 17 March 2007
2-d bar-coded SDLT1 Return failures
Question 59 – Authorising an agent to handle correspondence
Netherton SDLT processing centre
Schedules: when they are required
General Feedback
Stamp Taxes Online Internet pages
Paper copies of online returns
Stamp Taxes Online: practical arrangements for practitioners
Stamp Taxes Online: feedback
SDLT Online: – paying SDLT efficiently
SDLT Online :Accessing Local Authority Numbers and SDLT calculators

STAMP DUTY LAND TAX ("SDLT")

Meeting with Commercial Case Management Software Developers
New rates of interest on stamp taxes paid late and overpaid
Previous issues of the SDLT Practitioners' Newsletter
Quick Links

Issue 18   June 2007

Unscannable black and white (2D bar-coded) land transaction returns – change in approach.
Submitting returns beyond the due date: 'reasonable excuses' for 2D bar-coded returns.
'Effective date' – how to avoid making errors on SDLT 1 (question 4) for lease transactions.
Advice on: retaining copies of SDLT1 returns; and purchasers not signing blank returns.
Online SDLT6 guidance notes are the most up-to-date.
SDLT CD-ROM will be discontinued when remaining stocks run out.
Revised SDLT60 (used to notify land registries that no SDLT 1 is required)/Where to send an SDLT60
SDLT cheque payments: remember to quote Unique Transaction Reference Numbers.
Stamp Taxes Online – the paper trail is over!
Lease start date (question 17 SDLT 1 & question 19 SDLT 4)
Effective date warning message
Automated Registration to Title of Land (ARTL) – for Scotland only.
Latest SDLT improvement initiatives
SDLT on the web: what's available on the Stamp Taxes area?
Stamp Taxes reorganisation: Stamp Taxes' latest movements of work.
General feedback: have your say
Practitioners' News: back issues

Issue 19   November 2007

Stamp Taxes Online New enhancements
Printing and submitting the SDLT5 certificate
Local Authorities and government departments can now register
Transactions with 100 or more properties
How to set up 'Users' & 'Assistants'
Adding 'Company Details' to an HMRC return
Multiple properties
What to do if you don't activate your registration within 28 days
Shared equity lease transactions
Other issues SDLT6 Guidance Notes: how to use the new HTML version
CHAPS Payments
Interest on late paid SDLT
Priority Faxes
Stamp Taxes Helpline
Stamp Taxes Reorganisation
Previous issues of the SDLT Practitioners' Newsletter
Quick Links

STAMP DUTY LAND TAX ("SDLT")

Issue 20 February 2008

- Stamp Taxes Online New enhancements
- Printing and submitting the SDLT5 certificate
- Local Authorities and government departments can now register Transactions with 100 or more properties
- How to set up 'Users' & 'Assistants'
- Adding 'Company Details' to an HMRC return
- Multiple properties
- What to do if you don't activate your registration within 28 days
- Shared equity lease transactions
- Other issues SDLT6 Guidance Notes: how to use the new HTML version
- CHAPS Payments
- Interest on late paid SDLT
- Priority Faxes
- Stamp Taxes Helpline
- Stamp Taxes Reorganisation
- Previous issues of the SDLT Practitioners' Newsletter
- Quick Links

Telephone assistance is available from HMRC Stamp Taxes Enquiry Line 0845 603 0135 on weekdays between 08.30 and 17.00, except public holidays.

1.3. GENERAL INFORMATION

Notification:

The printed versions of the prescribed land transaction return forms are:

SDLT1	the main land transaction return form
SDLT2	this form is required where there are more than two purchasers or more than two vendors;
SDLT3	this form is required where additional information is needed to identify the property, or the transaction involves more than one property.
SDLT4	additional details must be given about the transaction including company purchaser, business acquisition and leases.

Completed returns should be returned to:

HM Revenue & Customs
Stamp Taxes/SDLT
Comben House
Farriers Way
Netherton
Merseyside
L30 4RN

By DX:
Rapid Data Capture Centre
DX: 725593
Bootle 9

Returns can also be submitted electronically via Stamp Taxes Online (www.hmrc.gov.uk/so/online/menu.htm).

Supplies of the various land transaction return forms can be obtained on-line or by telephone: HMRC Orderline – 0845 302 1472 – between 08.00 and 22.00 (open every day, except Christmas Day, Boxing Day and New Year's Day.

STAMP DUTY LAND TAX ("SDLT")

Notification requirements:

Leasehold property purchases where the lease is granted for seven years or more

HMRC does not have to be notified about the grant of a residential or non-residential lease where the lease is for seven years or more as long as:
- any premium is less than £40,000
- the annual rent is less than £1,000

HMRC does not have to be notified about the assignment or surrender of a residential or non-residential lease as long as both of the following apply:
- the lease was originally granted for seven years or more
- the chargeable consideration for the assignment or surrender is less than £40,000

Leasehold property purchases where the lease is granted for less than seven years

HMRC does not have to be notified about a residential or non-residential leasehold property transaction where the lease is granted for less than seven years provided the chargeable consideration does not include any amount which exceeds the relevant residential/non-residential SDLT threshold.

These amounts include:
- any premium and the net present value of any rent in the case of a new lease
- the consideration given for the assignment or surrender of an existing lease

Alternative property finance (e.g. Islamic Mortgages)

Where there are financial arrangements for property purchase involving transactions with the lending institution that are consequential to the main property transaction (for example, in order to comply with Sharia law), these consequential transactions are exempt from SDLT and do not need to be notified to HMRC.

In addition, the interest held by a financial institution as a result of an alternative finance mortgage is an 'exempt interest'. This means that there is no SDLT charge on dealings in such an interest or an interest derived from it (for example, the issue of or trading in sukuk-backed alternative finance assets) and no requirement for parties to these sorts of transactions to submit SDLT returns.

Transactions that do not represent a major interest in the land

There are numerous transfers of land or property which are below the zero rate threshold and do not represent a major interest. Examples include rights of way, drainage etc. These transactions do not need to be notified.

Assents and appropriations:

Section 300 Finance Act 2004 clarifies the position on assents and appropriations. The acquisition of property by a person in or towards satisfaction of his entitlement under or in relation to the will of a deceased person, or on the intestacy of a deceased person, is exempt from a charge to SDLT, unless

STAMP DUTY LAND TAX ("SDLT")

the person acquiring the property gives any consideration for it, other than the assumption of secured debt as defined in that section.

Identification plans:

Practitioners's Newsletter Issue 2 explains the situation. For example, a plan is not needed for domestic property including new housing developments (where properties are often referred to by plot numbers) but is required for development land; agricultural land; small 'garden' plots and where a boundary needs defining. The plan must show the scale (or the plan must be endorsed 'Not to Scale' if applicable); the reference number of the SDLT1 return (shown in the 'Reference' box on the payslip in the form); the address or description of the land as entered into the SDLT1 and the local authority code as entered into the SDLT1.

Time limits:

The land transaction return form must be delivered to HMRC by the "filing date"-which is 30 days after the "effective date" of the transaction. The Guidance Notes and other HMRC publications explain how the definition of "effective date" applies to:
- a completed transaction
- a contract that is substantially performed before completion and
- other situations, such as an option or a right of pre-emption.

1.4 "CHARGEABLE CONSIDERATION"

The Guidance Notes explain that there are many forms of consideration for land and although cash is the most common, SDLT is chargeable on the total of all forms of consideration in money or money's worth.

The following are examples of chargeable consideration as referred to in the Guidance Notes:
- "Debt" – this might be the satisfaction or release of debt due to the purchaser or owed by the vendor and/or the assumption of existing debt by the purchaser.
- "Building works" – this might arise where a purchaser agrees to carry out building works on land, other than that which is the subject of the land transaction or already owned by the purchaser.
- "Employment" – this might arise where the land transaction is entered into by reason of the purchaser's employment, or that of a person connected with the purchaser.
- "Other consideration"-this might arise where the consideration is an annuity payable for life, or in perpetuity, or for an indefinite period, or for a definite period exceeding 12 years.
- "Shares" – the Guidance Notes state that quoted and unquoted shares must be valued as at the effective date of the transaction.
- "Other land" (exchanges) – this might arise where a purchaser and vendor are exchanging land for other land. The Guidance Notes state that there are in effect, two separate transactions, each of which must be notified. An example (given in the Guidance Notes) is where two properties are exchanged, when the SDLT is

charged on the "market value" of the subject of the transaction, rather than on the consideration given.
- "Contingent" or "unascertained" consideration – this might be where a transaction provides for further consideration to be paid in the future depending on whether or not a specific future event takes place. An example, given in the Guidance Notes is where a further amount is to be paid if a purchaser is granted planning permission.
- "Restrictions, covenants or conditions affecting the value of the estate or interest transferred or granted" – the Guidance Notes explain that information should be supplied if any of these matters apply (historic or new), so that there is an effect on the amount of "chargeable consideration" or the rent payable. The Guidance Notes explain how this might apply where a vendor has a right to buy the property back at less than "market value", or where there are covenants in a lease restricting the use of a shop to a particular trade, or a house is subject to an "agricultural occupancy condition".

"Linked transactions":

The Guidance Notes explain the meaning of "linked transactions". This might arise where transactions form part of a single scheme, or arrangement, or series of transactions between the same vendor and purchaser or, in either case, between persons connected with them. The Guidance Notes include the following examples:
- a husband and wife are "connected";
- a person is "connected" with his or her brother or sister;
- a person is "connected" with a company that he or she controls; or
- two companies are "connected" if the same person controls both of them.

The Guidance Notes and other HMRC publications explain the notification requirements for "linked transactions" (including "linked leases") and that if transactions are linked the rate of SDLT depends upon the aggregate consideration.

An example is that of a man who buys a house for £240,000 and his wife buys the garden of the house for £20,000. Both purchases are from the same vendor as part of a single bargain. In that event SDLT is charged at 3% on both transactions (the rate currently applicable to the aggregate consideration of £260,000).

1.5 "DISADVANTAGED AREA RELIEF" AND OTHER RELIEFS AND EXEMPTIONS

Disadvantaged Areas Relief can reduce the amount of SDLT payable in areas designated by the government as 'disadvantaged'. It is currently only available for the residential element of mixed use (residential and non-residential) properties. Detailed information on Disadvantaged Area Relief, including which areas and properties Disadvantaged Areas Relief applies to, the current rates, and how to work out how much SDLT is payable if a property qualifies, can be found at www.hmrc.gov.uk/sdlt/reliefs-exemptions/disadvantaged-areas.htm.

HMRC provides a postcode search tool on its website, where the known postcode of a property can be used to help identify whether it falls within one of the disadvantaged areas.

STAMP DUTY LAND TAX ("SDLT")

Royal Mail provides postcode information at www.royalmail.com.uk or by phone at the Royal Mail Postcode Enquiry Line 08457 111 222.

The following are examples of other "reliefs" and "exemptions", but please refer to the online guide at www.hmrc.gov.uk/sdlt/reliefs-exemptions/overview.htm for details of the conditions that apply in each case:

- A part-exchange transaction involving a house-building company – this might apply where a house-building company acquires a dwelling from an individual in consideration of the same person buying a new dwelling from that company or where a house-building company uses an "unconnected company" to acquire an individual's dwelling.
- a transaction involving a company that provides "chain breaking assistance" – this might apply to a company whose trade consists of buying residential property for the purpose of preventing a chain of residential transactions from failing.
- A transaction involving companies that purchase residential property from personal representatives and then sell on such property.
- A transaction relating to relocation of employment.
- A "right to buy transaction" (including the grant of a lease under the "right to buy" legislation).
- A lease granted by a "registered social landlord".
- A transaction in connection with a divorce.
- A variation of a testamentary disposition carried out within two years of the deceased's death.

1.6 RATES OF SDLT ON THE "CHARGEABLE CONSIDERATION"

The following table sets out the rates of SDLT that apply to the "chargeable consideration" (an example being a transfer or conveyance of freehold land or an assignment of a lease). Please refer to 1.7 below for the rates of SDLT on the grant of a lease.

Rate	Land in disadvantaged areas- Residential	Land in disadvantaged areas – Non-residential	All other land in the UK – Residential	All other land in the UK – Non-residential
Zero	£0 – £150,000	£0 – £150,000	£0 – £125,000	£0 – £150,000
1%	Over £150,000 – £250,000	Over £150,000 – £250,000	Over £125,000 – £250,000	Over £150,000 – £250,000
3%	Over £250,000 – £500,000	Over £250,000 – £500,000	Over £250,000 – £500,000	Over £250,000 – £500,000
4%	Over £500,000	Over £500,000	Over £500,000	Over £500,000

Notes:
- SDLT is rounded down to the next whole pound.
- Any Value Added Tax payable on the chargeable consideration should be included in the SDLT calculations.

The SDLT threshold for land transactions consisting entirely of residential property is £175,000 for transactions with an effective date (i.e. completion) after 2 September 2008 and before 31 December 2009. Thus, no SDLT will be due where the chargeable consideration is £175,000 or less, and where the chargeable consideration is greater than £175,000 but no greater than £250,000, the rate of SDLT will be 1%.

STAMP DUTY LAND TAX ("SDLT")

1.7 SDLT ON THE GRANT OF A LEASE

SDLT on premium

The charging system (for both residential and non-residential property) is a slab system in which the entire consideration is charged at the applicable rate. For example, if the consideration is £300,000, SDLT is charged at 3% on the whole £300,000 and not just the amount in excess of £250,000.

In the case of a lease where the effective date fell before 12 March 2008 (including an agreement for lease that is substantially performed), and the average annual rent exceeded £600 per year, there was no 0% band available in respect of the non-rent consideration, and so an SDLT rate of at least 1% applied to the non-rent consideration. This '£600 rule' has been changed where the effective date is on or after 12 March 2008 so that the nil-rate band is available for any premium payable on:

- Non-residential leases where the annual rent is less than £1,000.
- All residential leases (irrespective of the annual rent amount).

The following rates of SDLT apply to the calculation of SDLT on a premium but see below for SDLT on the rental element:

Rate	Land in disadvan- taged areas- Residential	Land in disadvan- taged areas – Non- residential	All other land in the UK – Residential	All other land in the UK – Non- residential
Zero	£0 – £150,000	£0 – £150,000	£0 – £125,000	£0 – £150,000
1%	Over £150,000 – £250,000	Over £150,000 – £250,000	Over £125,000 – £250,000	Over £150,000 – £250,000
3%	Over £250,000 – £500,000	Over £250,000 – £500,000	Over £250,000 – £500,000	Over £250,000 – £500,000
4%	Over £500,000	Over £500,000	Over £500,000	Over £500,000

Notes:
- The SDLT due on the grant of a lease depends on the premium payable; the rent due under the lease and the term of the lease. The two elements are added together and entered onto the land transaction return as a total figure.
- SDLT is rounded down to the next whole pound.
- Any Value Added Tax payable on the chargeable consideration should be included in the SDLT calculations.

See 1.6 above for the position regarding residential property up to 31 December 2009.

SDLT on rent

Where the consideration includes rent, SDLT is charged on the net present value (NPV) of the rent over the term of the lease. A temporal discount of 3.5% is applied to the rents payable in each year of the lease (including the rent payable in the first year). This reflects the fact that rents to be received in the future have a lower value than rents received today.

HMRC provides a tool on its website to assist in calculating the net present value.

STAMP DUTY LAND TAX ("SDLT")

If that calculation tool is not used, the following statutory formula must be applied for the purposes of calculating the net present value:

$$NPV = \sum_{i=1}^{n} \frac{r_i}{(1+T)^i}$$

In the above formula:

- NPV   is the net present value
- r_i is the rent payable in the year
- i   is the first, second, third etc year of the term
- n   is the term of the lease
- T   is the "temporal discount" rate. This is applied to reflect the fact that future rental payments are of less value than current rental payments". At the date of publication of this guide the "temporal discount" rate to be used in the above formula is 3.5%. HM Treasury can amend that from time to time by regulations made pursuant to the SDLT legislation. The amended rate must be then be used in the above formula.

The following rates of SDLT apply to the calculation of SDLT on the net present rental value:

Net present value (NPV) of the rent **Residential land**	Rates of SDLT on the NPV
£0 to £125,000	0%
Over £125,000	1% – but see the Notes below

Net present value (NPV) of the rent **Non-residential land**	Rates of SDLT on the NPV
£0 to £150,000	0%
Over £150,000	1% – but see the Notes below

Notes:

- When calculating duty payable on the NPV of the lease – reduce the NPV calculation by the following *before* applying the 1% rate:–
  Residential – £125,000
  Non-residential – £150,000
- The SDLT due on the grant of a lease depends on the premium payable; the rent due under the lease and the term of the lease. The two elements are added together and entered onto the land transaction return as a total figure
- SDLT is rounded down to the next whole pound
- Any Value Added Tax payable on the chargeable consideration should be included in the SDLT calculations.

SDLT and 'abnormal' rent increases

The tenant of a lease must review every rent increase after the fifth year of the lease. Broadly speaking, if the rent has doubled, or more than doubled, since the fifth year it will be treated as an 'abnormal' rent increase and the lease owner must make a further SDLT return and pay any tax, or extra tax, due. This is the case even if the increase is under the terms of the lease, or a variation of it.

The only exception to this is where the original lease is a 'Stamp Duty lease' – a lease that was granted before SDLT was introduced on 1 December 2003. In this case, no SDLT is payable.

There is an online abnormal rent increase calculator at www.hmrc.gov.uk/tools/stamps/abnormalrentcalculator.htm which can be used to help work out whether a rent increase is abnormal and, if it is, how much SDLT is payable, if any. If any SDLT is payable the tenant must write to the Birmingham Stamp Office within 30 days of the review date telling them the revised amount and enclosing any extra payment due. If the review shows that there had originally been an overestimation of the rent and too much SDLT had been paid, the tenant can write to claim a refund.

2. LAND REGISTRY

The information contained in this section of the guide is based on the law and practice under the Land Registration Act 2002 and the Land Registration Rules 2003, effective from 13 October 2003. For information on Land Registry fees, see Part 2.4 below.

The Land Registration (Amendment) Rules 2008 (SI 2008/1919) came into force on 10 November 2008, with the exception of Paragraph 40 of Schedule 1 (new rule 111) dealing with certificates of registration of company charges, which will come into force when section 869 of the Companies Act 2006 comes into force). The Land Registration (Amendment) Rules 2008 amend the Land Registration Rules 2003. The amendments are miscellaneous and follow a general review of the principal rules carried out by Land Registry.

For applications requiring the use of forms AP1, DS2 and FR1 received at the Land Registry on or after 10 November 2008 it is mandatory to use the form as amended by the Land Registration (Amendment) Rules 2008. With all other forms the unamended version may be used if its use is expressly required by an agreement entered into at least three months before 10 November 2008, by a court order or by or under an enactment.

2.1 LAND REGISTRY OFFICES

To find out which Land Registry Office is the "proper office" for a specific administrative area, please compare the number next to each Land Registry Office as listed below against the respective numbers in the second column of the list of local authorities in Part 3 of this guide. Land Registry will reject applications that are sent to the wrong office (see Rule 15(3) of the Land Registration Rules 2003). Land Registry does not deem an application to have been received until it reaches the "proper office". For more information on these subjects please refer to Land Registry Practice Guides 49 and 51.

Land Registry Practice Guide 44 explains the Registry's requirements and the services that are available when using Land Registry's *"Fax facilities"*. Each Practice Guide can be obtained from a Land Registry Customer Information Centre (at any Land Registry Office) or can be viewed at or downloaded from www.landregistry.gov.uk

LAND REGISTRY

Name of Land Registry Office

1. **Birkenhead (Old Market)**
   Old Market House
   Hamilton Street
   Birkenhead
   Merseyside CH41 5FL
   Tel: 0151 473 1110
   Fax: 0151 473 0251
   DX 14300 Birkenhead (3)

2. **Birkenhead (Rosebrae)**
   Rosebrae Court
   Woodside Ferry Approach
   Birkenhead
   Merseyside CH41 6DU
   Tel: 0151 472 6666
   Fax: 0151 472 6789
   DX 24270 Birkenhead (4)

3. **Coventry**
   Leigh Court
   Torrington Avenue
   Tile Hill
   Coventry CV4 9XZ
   Tel: 024 7686 0860
   Fax: 024 7686 0021
   DX 18900 Coventry (3)

4. **Croydon**
   Trafalgar House
   1 Bedford Park
   Croydon CR0 2QA
   Tel: 020 8781 9100
   Fax: 020 8781 9110
   DX 2699 Croydon (3)

5. **Durham**
   Southfield House
   Southfield Way
   Durham DH1 5TR
   Tel: 0191 301 3500
   Fax: 0191 301 0020
   DX 60200 Durham (3)

6. **Gloucester**
   Twyver House
   Bruton Way
   Gloucester GL1 1DQ
   Tel: 01452 511111
   Fax: 01452 510050
   DX 7599 Gloucester (3)

7. **Kingston upon Hull**
   Earle House
   Colonial Street
   Hull HU2 8JN
   Tel: 01482 223244
   Fax: 01482 224278
   DX 26700 Hull (4)

8. **Fylde (Wrea Brook Court)**
   Wrea Brook Court
   Lytham Road
   Warton
   Preston PR4 1TE
   Tel: 01772 836700
   Fax: 01772 836970
   DX 721560 Lytham (6)

9. **Leicester**
   Westbridge Place
   Leicester LE1 5DR
   Tel: 0116 265 4000
   Fax: 0116 265 4008
   DX 11900 Leicester (5)

10. **Fylde (Birkenhead House)**
    Birkenhead House
    East Beach
    Lytham St Annes FY8 5AB
    Tel: 01253 849849
    Fax: 01253 840001
    DX 14500 Lytham St Annes (3)

11. **Nottingham (East)**
    Robins Wood Road
    Nottingham NG8 3RQ
    Tel: 0115 906 5353
    Fax: 0115 936 0036
    DX 716126 Nottingham (26)

12. **Nottingham (West)**
    Chalfont Drive
    Nottingham NG8 3RN
    Tel: 0115 935 1166
    Fax: 0115 935 0038
    DX 10298 Nottingham (3)

13. **Peterborough**
    Touthill Close
    City Road
    Peterborough PE1 1XN
    Tel: 01733 288288
    Fax: 01733 280022
    DX 12598 Peterborough (4)

14. **Plymouth**
    Plumer House
    Tailyour Road
    Crownhill
    Plymouth PL6 5HY
    Tel: 01752 636000
    Fax: 01752 636161
    DX 8299 Plymouth (4)

15. **Portsmouth**
    St Andrew's Court
    St Michael's Road
    Portsmouth PO1 2JH
    Tel: 023 9276 8888
    Fax: 023 9276 8768
    DX 83550 Portsmouth (2)

16. **Stevenage**
    Brickdale House
    Swingate
    Stevenage
    Herts SG1 1XG
    Tel: 01438 788888
    Fax: 01438 785460
    DX 6099 Stevenage (2)

17. **Swansea**
    Ty Bryn Glas
    High Street
    Swansea SA1 1PW
    Tel: 01792 458877
    Fax: 01792 473236
    DX 33700 Swansea (12)

18. **Telford**
    Parkside Court
    Hall Park Way
    Telford TF3 4LR
    Tel: 01952 290355
    Fax: 01952 290356
    DX 28100 Telford (2)

LAND REGISTRY

19. Tunbridge Wells
Forest Court
Forest Road
Tunbridge Wells
Kent TN2 5AQ
Tel: 01892 510015
Fax: 01892 510032
DX 3999 Tunbridge Wells (2)

20. Wales
Ty Cwm Tawe
Phoenix Way
Llansamlet
Swansea SA7 9FQ
Tel: 01792 355000
Fax: 01792 355055
DX 82800 Swansea (2)

21. Weymouth
Melcombe Court
1 Cumberland Drive
Weymouth
Dorset DT4 9TT
Tel: 01305 363636
Fax: 01305 363646
DX 8799 Weymouth (2)

Land Registry Head Office:
Lincoln's Inn Fields
London WC2A 3PH
DX 1098 London/Chancery Lane WC2
Tel: 020 7917 8888
Fax: 020 7955 0110 (for correspondence only)
Applications and searches should not be sent to Land Registry Head Office.
Website: www.landregistry.gov.uk

Land Registry Customer Information Centres

Every Land Registry Office has a Customer Information Centre where the "public counter" is located, and which is open from 08.30 to 18.00 Mondays to Fridays (except on public holidays).

See "Information Services Applications" in Part 2.4 of this guide for more information about the types of oral application that can be made (and the fees) at a Customer Information Centre.

Land Registry "Telephone Services"

See Land Registry Practice Guide 61 and "Information Services Applications" in Part 2.4 of this guide for more information about the specific telephone applications and searches that credit account holders can make.

The dedicated Telephone Service numbers for Land Registry credit account holders are:

Telephone Services number for England   0844 892 0307
For Welsh Language Service – telephone 0844 892 0308

Land Registry Direct

See Part 14 of this guide for more information about the types of application that can be made by subscribers to this service and the fees payable.

2.2 LAND REGISTRY "PRACTICE GUIDES"

Land Registry publishes detailed Practice Guides for conveyancers. These cover a range of topics on land registration practice and procedures.

Any Customer Information Centre can supply printed copies of the Practice Guides or the Guides can be viewed at or downloaded from www.landregistry.gov.uk

Practice Guide	Title
PG1	First Registrations
PG2	First registration of title where deeds have been lost or destroyed
PG3	Cautions against first registration
PG4	Adverse possession of registered land under the new provisions of the Land Registration Act 2002

LAND REGISTRY

PG5	Adverse possession of unregistered land and transitional provisions for registered land in the Land Registration Act 2002
PG005 Flyer	Adverse possession of unregistered land and transitional provisions for registered land in the Land Registration Act 2002
PG6	Devolution on the death of a registered proprietor
PG7	Entry of price paid or value stated on the register
PG8	Execution of deeds
PG9	Powers of attorney and registered land
PG10	Official searches of the Index Map
PG11	Inspection and applications for official copies
PG12	Official searches and outline applications
PG13	Official searches of the index of relating franchises and manors
PG14	Charities
PG15	Overriding interests and their disclosure
PG16	Profits a prendre in gross
PG17	Souvenir Land
PG18	Franchises
PG19	Notices, restrictions and the protection of third party interest in the register
PG20	Applications under the Family Law Act 1996
PG21	Using transfer forms for less straightforward transactions
PG22	Manors
PG23	Electronic lodgement of applications to change the register
PG24	Private trusts of land
PG25	Leases – when to register
PG26	Leases – determination
PG26 – Addendum	Leases Determination
PG27	The Leasehold Reform Legislation
PG28	Extension of leases
PG29	Registration of legal charges and deeds of variation of charge
PG30	Approval of mortgage documentation
PG31	Discharges of charges
PG32	Applications affecting one or more Land Registry Office
PG33	Large scale applications (calculation of fees)
PG34	Personal insolvency
PG35	Corporate insolvency
PG36	Administration and receivership
PG37	Objections and disputes – a guide to Land Registry practice and procedures
PG38	Costs
PG39	Rectification and indemnity
PG40	Land Registry plans: a summary of Land Registry plan records, pre-registration requirements, other plans related services
PG41	Developing estates – registration services
PG41-S1	Developing estates – registration services Supplement 1: Estate Boundary Approval
PG41-S2	Developing estates – registration services Supplement 2: Estate Plan Approval
PG41-S3	Developing estates – registration services Supplement 3: Approval of draft transfers and leases
PG41-S4	Developing estates – registration services Supplement 4: Plot sales – transfers and leases
PG41-S5	Developing estates – registration services Supplement 5: Detailed plan requirements and surveying specifications – guidance for surveyors

LAND REGISTRY

PG41-S6	Developing estates – registration services Supplement 6: Voluntary application to note overriding interests
PG42	Upgrading the class of title
PG43	Applications in connection with court proceedings, insolvency and tax liability
PG44	Fax facilities
PG45	Receiving and replying to notices by e-mail
PG46	Land Registry forms
PG47	Transfers of public housing estates
PG48	Implied covenants
PG49	Rejection of applications for registration
PG50	Requisition and cancellation procedures
PG50 – Addendum	Requisition and cancellation procedures
PG51	Areas served by Land Registry Offices
PG52	Easements claimed by prescription
PG53	Scheme Titles
PG54	Acquisition of land by General Vesting Declaration under the Compulsory Purchase (Vesting Declarations) Act 1981
PG55	Address for service
PG56	Formal apportionment and redemption of a rent or a rentcharge that affects a registered estate
PG57	Exempting documents from the general right to inspect and copy
PG58	Land Registry's Welsh Language Scheme – register format
PG59	Receiving and replying to acquisitions by e-mail
PG60	Commonhold
PG60 – Addendum	Commonhold
PG61	Telephone Services (credit account holders only)
PG62	Easements
PG63	Land Charges – Applications for registration, official search, office copy and cancellation.
PG64	Prescribed clauses leases
PG64 – Addendum	Prescribed clauses leases – addendum to Practice Guide 64
PG65	Registration of mines and minerals
PG66	Overriding interests losing automatic protection in 2013
PG67	Evidence of identity-conveyancers

2.3 APPLICATION AND SEARCH FORMS

Title of form	Description
ACD	Application for approval of a standard form of charge deed and allocation of official Land Registry reference
ADV1	Application for registration of a person in adverse possession under Schedule 6 to the Land Registration Act 2002
ADV2	Application to be registered as a person to be notified of an application for adverse possession
AN1	Application to enter an agreed notice
AP1	Application to change the register
AS1	Assent of whole of registered title(s)
AS2	Assent of charge
AS3	Assent of part of registered title(s)
CC	Entry of a note of consolidation of charges
CCD	Application to cancel a caution against dealings
CCT	Application to cancel a caution against first registration
CH1	Legal charge of a registered estate
CH2	Application to enter an obligation to make further advances

LAND REGISTRY

CH3	Application to note agreed maximum amount of security
CIT	Application in connection with court proceedings, insolvency and tax liability
CM1	Application to register a freehold estate in commonhold land
CM2	Application for the freehold estate to cease to be registered as a freehold estate in commonhold land during the transitional period
CM3	Application for the registration of an amended commonhold community statement and/or altered memorandum and articles of association
CM4	Application to add land to a commonhold registration
CM5	Application for the termination of a commonhold registration
CM6	Application for the registration of a successor commonhold association
CN1	Application to cancel notice (other than a unilateral notice)
COE	Notification of change of extent of a commonhold unit over which there is a registered charge
CON1	Consent to the registration of land as a commonhold estate
CON2	Consent to an application for the freehold estate to cease to be registered in commonhold land during the transitional period
COV	Application for registration with unit-holders
CS	Continuation sheet for use with application and disposition forms
CT1	Caution against First Registration
DB	Application to determine the exact line of a boundary
DI	Disclosable overriding interests
DJP	Application to remove from the register the name of a deceased joint proprietor
DL	List of documents
DS1	Cancellation of entries relating to a registered charge
DS2	Application to cancel entries relating to a registered charge
DS2E	Application to cancel entries relating to a registered charge
DS3	Release of part of the land from a registered charge
EX1	Application for the registrar to designate a document as an exempt information document
EX1A	Reasons for exemption in support of an application to designate a document as an exempt information document
EX2	Application for official copy of an exempt information document
EX3	Application to remove the designation of a document as an exempt information document
FR1	First Registration application
HC1	Application for copies of historical edition(s) of the register/title plan held in electronic form
HR1	Application for registration of a notice of home rights
HR2	Application for renewal of registration in respect of home rights
HR3	Application by mortgagee for official search in respect of home rights
HR4	Cancellation of a home rights notice

LAND REGISTRY

ID1	Evidence of identity for a private individual
ID2	Evidence of identity for a corporate body
OC1	Application for official copies of register/plan or certificate in Form CI
OC2	Application for official copies of documents only
OS1	Application by purchaser for official search with priority of the whole of the land in a registered title or a pending first registration application
OS2	Application by purchaser for official search with priority of part of the land in a registered title or a pending first registration application
OS3	Application for official search without priority of the land in a registered title
PIC	Application for a personal inspection under section 66 of the Land Registration Act 2002
PN1	Application for a search in the Index of Proprietors' Names
PRD1	Request for the production of documents
RD1	Request for the return of original documents
RX1	Application to enter a restriction
RX2	Application for an order that a restriction be disapplied or modified
RX3	Application to cancel a restriction
RX4	Application to withdraw a restriction
SC	Application for noting the overriding priority of a statutory charge
SEV	Application to enter Form A restriction on severance of joint tenancy by agreement or notice
SIF	Application for an official search of the index of relating franchises and manors
SIM	Application for an official search of the index map
SR1	Notice of surrender of development rights
ST1	Statement of truth in support of an application for registration based upon adverse possession
ST2	Statement of truth in support of an application based upon adverse possession of a rentcharge
ST3	Statement of truth in support of an application for registration of land based upon lost or destroyed title deeds
ST4	Statement of truth in support of an application for registration and/or noting of a prescriptive easements
TP1	Transfer of part of registered title(s)
TP2	Transfer of part of registered title(s) under power of sale
TR1	Transfer of whole of registered title(s)
TR2	Transfer of whole of registered title(s) under power of sale
TR4	Transfer of a charge or portfolio of charges
TR5	Transfer of portfolio of titles (whole or part)
UN1	Application to enter a unilateral notice
UN2	Application to remove a unilateral notice
UN3	Application to be registered as beneficiary of an existing unilateral notice
UN4	Application for the cancellation of a unilateral notice by a person who is (or is entitled to be) the registered proprietor
	Application for upgrading of title
	Application to withdraw a caution
	Prescribed clauses contained in Schedule 1A to the Land Registration Rules 2003

2.4 LAND REGISTRY FEES

The Land Registration Fee Order 2009 applies to fees payable for applications and searches received at Land Registry offices on or after 6 July 2009.

The fee information set out below is a summary.

Further fee information can be obtained from any Customer Information Centre or can be viewed at or downloaded from www.landregistry.gov.uk

Land Registry also provides an "online fee calculator" – at www.landregistry.gov.uk.

Contact details:

Credit Accounts Information:

Accounts Section
Land Registry Land Charges Department
Plumer House
Tailyour Road
Crownhill
Plymouth PL6 5HY
DX 8249 Plymouth (3)
Tel: 01752 636666

Telephone Services (available only to credit account holders):

Contact the Customer Service Manager at any Land Registry office.
Website: www.landregistry.gov.uk

Land Registry Direct (available only to credit account holders):

Land Registry e-Services Delivery
Touthill Close
City Road
Peterborough PE1 1XN
DX 12598 Peterborough 4
Tel: 0870 0100299
E-mail: admin@landregistrydirect.gov.uk
Website: www.landregistrydirect.gov.uk

National Land Information Service:

NLIS
Local Government Information House
Layden House
76–86 Turnmill Street
London EC1M 5LG
Tel: 01279 451625

Applications are available on the terms set out in the user agreement, which can be viewed at www.nlis.org.uk. See Part 15 of this guide for more information about NLIS.

Additional information about fees:

Value Added Tax

When assessing value under either Scale 1 or Scale 2, fees must be paid on the VAT-inclusive consideration or rent. Land Registry fees are not subject to VAT.

Payment of fees

Payment for services and substantive applications can be made by cheque or postal order – payable to "L…

Credit accounts can be used by arrangement.

Fee information is available on the Land Registry www.landregistry.gov.uk

LAND REGISTRY

Registration Services Fees

The following applies to all registration services applications received at Land Registry offices on or after 6 July 2009.

It is a summary only. For further details see the Land Registration Fee Order 2009.

An application may be cancelled if the correct fee is not paid. If you are unsure of the fee, you should contact Land Registry for advice.

SCALE 1 of the Land Registration Fee Order 2009:
Articles 2 and 3. Reduced by 25% for voluntary first registration.

Amount or value £	Fee £	Reduced fee for voluntary registration £
0-50,000	50	40
50,001-80,000	80	60
80,001-100,000	130	100
100,001-200,000	200	150
200,001-500,000	280	210
500,001-1,000,000	550	410
1,000,001 and over	920	690

Use Scale 1 for:
- **The first registration of a freehold or leasehold estate, franchise or profit**
  If made within one year of an open market sale, base the fee on the consideration (plus the amount outstanding under any continuing charge).
  However, for the following first registrations the fee is payable on the full current open market value of the estate:
    - Assents;
    - Exchanges;
    - First mortgages;
    - First registrations more than one year old;
    - Franchises;
    - Profits;
    - Transfers by way of gift;
    - Transfers of a share.
- **The registration of the grant of a lease**
  See Leases section below
- **The registration of a transfer of a registered estate for monetary consideration**
  The fee is payable on the consideration.
- **The registration of a surrender of a leasehold estate for monetary consideration**
  See Leases section below

LE 2 of the Land Registration Fee Order 2009:
and 5. Do not use for any first registration.

alue	Fee £
	50
	70
	90
	130
	260

- **A transfer of a registered estate otherwise than for monetary consideration**
  Assess the fee on the value of the estate, less the amount outstanding on any continuing registered charge. Where a transfer not for value gives effect to the transfer of a share in a registered estate, the fee is payable on the value of that share.
- **A surrender of a registered leasehold estate otherwise than for monetary consideration**
  See Leases section below
- **A transfer of a registered charge**
  The fee is payable on the consideration, or, where the transfer is not for value, on the amount secured by the charge at the time of the transfer.
  Where a transfer not for value gives effect to the transfer of a share in a registered charge, the fee is payable on the value of that share.
- **A charge**
  See Charges section below.
- **Other applications affecting registered estates**
  The fee for the following is payable on the value of the estate less the amount of any continuing registered charge:
    - a transfer of a registered estate by operation of law on death or bankruptcy, of an individual proprietor;
    - an assent of a registered estate (including a vesting assent);
    - an appropriation of a registered estate;
    - a vesting order or declaration;
    - an alteration of the register;
    - a transfer of a registered estate made pursuant to an order of the Court (under the Matrimonial Causes Act 1973 or the Civil Partnership Act 2004).

Charges of registered land
Use Scale 2.

Fees payable:
- where the charge secures a fixed amount, base the fee on that amount;
- where the charge secures further advances and the maximum amount that can be advanced or owed at any one time is limited, base the fee on the maximum amount;
- where the charge secures further advances and the total amount that can be advanced or owed at any one time is not limited, base the fee on the value of the property charged;
- where the charge is by way of additional or substituted security or by way of guarantee, base the fee on the lesser of:
    - the amount secured or guaranteed, or
    - the value of the property charged;
- where the charge secures an obligation or liability which is contingent upon the happening of a future event, base the fee on:
    - the maximum amount or value of the obligation, or
    - if that maximum amount is great[er] value of the property charged by the charge, or cannot be time of the application, the property charged.

No fee is payable for:
- a charge which accompanies a sca[le] under which the chargor becomes t[he] proprietor of the land;

LAND REGISTRY

- a charge which is lodged before the completion of an application for compulsory first registration, or for the registration of a transfer of registered land.

An application to register a charge that does not accompany, but is lodged before completion of, a voluntary first registration, is not exempt from a Scale 2 fee.

Leases:
Use Scale 1 for:
- **Registration**
  The fee for the registration of a lease (whether or not it is a registrable disposition) by the original lessee, or his personal representative, is payable:
  - on an amount equal to the sum of the premium and the rent; or
  - if there is no premium, on the amount of any quantifiable rent; or
  - if there is no premium and either there is no rent or the rent cannot be quantified, on the value of the lease (assessed under article 7 of the Land Registration Fee Order 2009) – subject to a minimum fee of £50.

"**Rent**" means the largest amount of annual rent the lease reserves within the first five years of its term that can be quantified at the time an application to register the lease is made.

- **Determination**
  For cancellation of an entry of notice of an unregistered lease on surrender, effluxion of time or forfeiture, the fee is based on the value of the lease immediately prior to its determination.

  For cancellation of an entry of notice of an unregistered lease on merger for:
  - no monetary consideration, the fee is based on the value of the lease immediately prior to its merger;
  - a monetary consideration, the fee is payable on the consideration.

  If the reversionary title is being transferred to the tenant, a Scale 1 fee is also payable on the transfer.

- **Surrender of a registered lease**
  The fee is based on the monetary consideration.

  No fee is payable to register the surrender of a registered lease where a scale fee is paid for the registration of a new lease of substantially the same property and the registered proprietor remains the same.

Use Scale 2 for a surrender of a lease other than for monetary consideration. The fee is based on the value of the lease prior to its surrender.

Exemptions

Under Schedule 4, the following applications are exempt from payment of a fee:
(1) Reflecting a change in the name, address or description of a registered proprietor or other person referred to in the register, or in the cautions register, or changing the description of a property;
(2) Giving effect in the register to a change of proprietor where the registered estate or the registered charge, as the case may be, has become vested without further assurance (other than on the death or bankruptcy of a proprietor) in some person by the operation of any statute (other than the Act),

LAND REGISTRY

    statutory instrument or scheme taking effect under any statute or statutory instrument;
(3) Registering the surrender of a registered leasehold estate where the surrender is consideration or part consideration for the grant of a new lease to the registered proprietor of substantially the same premises as were comprised in the surrendered lease and where a scale fee is paid for the registration of the new lease;
(4) Registering a discharge of a registered charge;
(5) Registering a home rights notice, or renewal of such a notice, or renewal of a home rights caution under the Family Law Act 1996;
(6) Entering in the register the death of a joint proprietor;
(7) Cancelling the registration of a notice, (other than a notice in respect of an unregistered lease or unregistered rentcharge), caution against first registration, caution against dealings, including a withdrawal of a deposit or intended deposit, inhibition, restriction, or note;
(8) The removal of the designation of a document as an exempt information document;
(9) Approving an estate layout plan or any draft document with or without a plan;
(10) An order by the registrar (other than an order under section 41(2) of the Land Registration Act 2002);
(11) Deregistering a manor;
(12) An entry in the register of a note of the dissolution of a corporation;
(13) Registering a restriction in Form A in Schedule 4 to the Land Registration Rules 2003;
(14) An application for day list information on any one occasion from a remote terminal;
(15) An application to lodge a caution against first registration or to make a register entry where in either case the application relates to rights in respect of the repair of a church chancel.

Fixed Fees

The following applications attract a fixed fee:

Part 1

1.	Standard restrictions; most notices; new or additional beneficiaries of a unilateral notice.	Up to three titles	£50
	NB No fee is payable if, for each registered title affected, the application is accompanied by a scale fee application or another application attracting a fee under this same paragraph, i.e. Schedule 3, Part 1(1).	Each additional title	£25
2.	Non-standard restrictions	Per title	£100
3.	Caution against first registration (other than one under s 117(2)(a) of the Land Registration Act 2002)		£50
4.	Alter a cautions register	Per register	£50
5.	*Closing a leasehold or rentcharge title (not on surrender) (for fees on surrender, see Leases section above)	Per title	£50
6.	*Upgrading a title		£50
7.	*Cancelling notice of an unregistered rentcharge	Per title	£50
8.	*Entry or removal of a record of a defect under s 64(1) of the Land Registration Act 2002		£50
9.	Outline application delivered: (a) by means of a remote terminal (b) by any other means		£3 £6

LAND REGISTRY

Most of the services referred to above are also available electronically, through Land Registry Direct or the National Land Information Service – please contact each service provider. See Parts 14 and 15 of this guide.

2.5. LAND CHARGES DEPARTMENT

Land Registry Practice Guide 63 – "Land Charges – Applications for registration, official search, office copy and cancellation" provides detailed information about applications made to Land Registry *Land Charges Department*.

General correspondence
Address this to:
The Superintendent
Land Charges Department
Plumer House
Tailyour Road
Plymouth PL6 5HY
DX 8249 Plymouth (3)

Telephone numbers at Land Charges Department (between 09.00 and 17.00 hours Monday to Friday, excluding public holidays):

General enquiries	01752 636 666
Agricultural Credits enquiries	01752 636 628
Cancellation enquiries	01752 636 626
Office Copy enquiries	01752 636 629
Land Charges registration enquiries – general	01752 636 634
Land Charges registration enquiries – bankruptcy	01752 636 616
Official search enquiries	01752 636 601
Credit accounts enquiries	01752 636 690

Land Charges applications and searches made through "Telephone Services" – see Land Registry Practice Guide 63 for detailed information:

Telephone Services for England	08709 088 063
For Welsh Language Service – telephone	08709 088 069

The above numbers must not be used for any other telephone enquiries.

Land Charges Department applications and searches

Land Registry Practice Guide 63 contains detailed information about the different methods of application and search.

"Paper" applications using an official Land Charges form (see the list below) should be sent by post, DX or by hand delivery to:
Land Charges Department
Plumer House
Tailyour Road
Crownhill
Plymouth PL6 5HY
DX 8249 Plymouth (3)

The fee for a paper application for a K15 or K16 Official Search is £1 per name. The fee for the other types of paper application listed below is £1 in each case – except where marked * in the following list (when no fee applies).

The fees are those prescribed by the Land Charges Fees Rules 1990 and the Land Charges Fees (Amendment) Rules 1994:

Form	Nature and use
K1	Registration of a land charge
K2	Registration of a land charge of Class F

LAND REGISTRY

K3	Registration of a pending land action
K4	Registration of a writ or order
K5	Registration of a deed of arrangement
K6	Registration of a priority notice
K7	Renewal of a registration of a land charge (except Class F)
K8	Renewal of a registration of a land charge of Class F
K9	Rectification of an entry in the register
K10	Continuation of an application
K11	Cancellation of an entry (except Class F)
K12	Cancellation of an entry in the register under special direction of the Registrar
K13	Cancellation of a land charge of Class F
K14	Declaration in support of an application for registration or rectification
K15	Official search (full)
K16	Official search (bankruptcy only)
K17*	Certificate of result of search (no subsisting entries)*
K18*	Certificate of result of search (entries revealed)*
K19	Application for an office copy of an entry in the register
K20	Application for a certificate of cancellation of an entry
K22*	Acknowledgement of an application*
K23*	Statement of account*

A "fax" application (available to Credit Account holders only) can be made by faxing the following official Land Charges forms to:

Land Charges Department Fax number – 01752 636 699

The fax facility is available between 08.00 and 16.00 hours Monday to Friday (except public holidays).

No other telephone or fax number should be used. The fees for applications made by fax are:

K15	(full Land Charges Search)	£2.00 per name
K16	(bankruptcy only search)	£2.00 per name
K19	(office copy of an entry including plan)	£1.00 per name

An "oral" application can be made by personal attendance at the Customer Information Centre at the Land Charges Department Plymouth (see above). This service is available between 08.30 and 18.00 hours Monday to Friday (except public holidays). For further information telephone 01752 636 666.

The fee is in each case the same as for a paper application.

Other methods of making Land Charges applications:

Some Land Charges applications can be made through:
- Land Registry Direct (a service available to Credit Account holders only). Subscribers to the service will be aware of the services and fees. For further information see Part 14 of this guide.
- National Land Information Service (NLIS). Details are set out in the user agreement, which can be viewed at www.nlis.org.uk. For further information see Part 15 of this guide.

3. LOCAL LAND CHARGES – SEARCHES AND ENQUIRIES (including a list of local authorities)

CON 29 (2007) was introduced with effect from 1 August 2007 and replaces CON 29 (2002). It is divided into two forms, both of which must be submitted in duplicate:

* CON 29R Enquiries of Local Authority (2007) which contains standard questions that should be raised in every case.

* CON 29O Optional Enquiries of Local Authority (2007). These enquiries are optional and should be asked if they are considered relevant to a transaction.

Please contact the relevant local authority listed below for details of the fees.

The following is an alphabetical list of local authorities, websites and telephone numbers as at the date of publication of this guide. The number immediately following the local authority name corresponds to the number against each Land Registry Office address as listed in Part 2.1 of this guide, being the proper office for lodging applications for registration in that particular area.

Please see part 22 of this guide for telephone numbers of other organisations.

Authority	No.	Website	Telephone
Adur District Council	15	www.adur.gov.uk	01273 263 000
Allerdale Borough Council	5	www.allerdale.gov.uk	01900 702 702
Amber Valley Borough Council	12	www.ambervalley.gov.uk	01773 570 222
Arun District Council	15	www.arun.gov.uk	01903 737 500
Ashfield District Council	11	www.ashfield-dc.gov.uk	01623 450 000
Ashford Borough Council	19	www.ashford.gov.uk	01233 331 111
Aylesbury Vale District Council	9	www.aylesburyvaledc.gov.uk	01296 585 858
Babergh District Council	7	www.babergh-south-suffolk.gov.uk	01473 822 801
Barking and Dagenham London Borough Council	16	www.barking-dagenham.gov.uk	020 8592 4500
Barnet London Borough Council	17	www.barnet.gov.uk	020 8359 2277
Barnsley Metropolitan Borough Council	11	www.barnsley.gov.uk	01226 770 770
Barrow in Furness Borough Council	5	www.barrowbc.gov.uk	01229 894 900
Basildon District Council	13	www.basildon.gov.uk	01268 533 333
Basingstoke and Deane Borough Council	21	www.basingstoke.gov.uk	01256 844 844
Bassetlaw District Council	11	www.bassetlaw.gov.uk	01909 533 533
Bath and North East Somerset Council	14	www.bathnes.gov.uk	01225 477 000
Bedford Borough Council	13	www.bedford.gov.uk	01234 267 422
Bexley London Borough Council	4	www.bexley.gov.uk	020 8303 7777
Birmingham City Council	3	www.birmingham.gov.uk	01213 031 111
Blaby District Council	9	www.blaby.gov.uk	01162 750 555
Blackburn with Darwen Borough Council	8	www.blackburn.gov.uk	01254 585 585
Blackpool Borough Council	8	www.blackpool.gov.uk	01253 477 477
Blaenau Gwent County Borough Council	20	www.blaenau-gwent.gov.uk	01495 350 555
Bolsover District Council	12	www.bolsover.gov.uk	01246 242 424
Bolton Metropolitan Borough Council	10	www.bolton.gov.uk	01204 333 333
Boston Borough Council	7	www.boston.gov.uk	01205 314 200
Bournemouth Borough Council	21	www.bournemouth.gov.uk	01202 451 451
Bracknell Forest Borough Council	6	www.bracknell-forest.gov.uk	01344 352 000
City of Bradford Metropolitan District Council	12	www.bradford.gov.uk	01274 431 000
Braintree District Council	13	www.braintree.gov.uk	01376 552 525
Breckland District Council	7	www.breckland.gov.uk	01362 656 870
Brent London Borough Council	17	www.brent.gov.uk	020 8937 1234
Brentwood Borough Council	13	www.brentwood-council.gov.uk	01277 312 500
Bridgend County Borough Council	20	www.bridgend.gov.uk	01656 643 643
Brighton & Hove City Council	15	www.brighton-hove.gov.uk	01273 290 000
Bristol City Council	6	www.bristol.gov.uk	01179 222 000
Broadland District Council	7	www.broadland.gov.uk	01603 431 133
Bromley London Borough Council	4	www.bromley.gov.uk	020 8464 3333
Bromsgrove District Council	3	www.bromsgrove.gov.uk	01527 873 232

LOCAL LAND CHARGES SEARCHES & ENQUIRIES

Council		Website	Phone
Broxbourne Borough Council	16	www.broxbourne.gov.uk	01992 785 555
Broxtowe Borough Council	11	www.broxtowe.gov.uk	01159 177 777
Burnley Borough Council	8	www.burnley.gov.uk	01282 425 011
Bury Metropolitan Borough Council	10	www.bury.gov.uk	01612 535 000
Caerphilly County Borough Council	20	www.caerphilly.gov.uk	01443 815 588
Calderdale Metropolitan Borough Council	12	www.calderdale.gov.uk	01422 357 257
Cambridge City Council	13	www.cambridge.gov.uk	01223 457 000
Camden London Borough Council	4	www.camden.gov.uk	020 7278 4444
Cannock Chase District Council	1	www.cannockchasedc.gov.uk	01543 462 621
Canterbury City Council	19	www.canterbury.gov.uk	01227 862 000
Cardiff Council	20	www.cardiff.gov.uk	029 2087 2087
Carlisle City Council	5	www.carlisle.gov.uk	01228 817 000
Carmarthenshire County Council	20	www.sirgaerfyrddin.gov.uk	01267 234 567
Castle Point Borough Council	13	www.castlepoint.gov.uk	01268 882 200
Central Bedfordshire Council	13	www.centralbedfordshire.gov.uk	0300 300 8000
Ceredigion County Council	20	www.ceredigion.gov.uk	01545 570 881
Charnwood Borough Council	9	www.charnwood.gov.uk	01509 263 151
Chelmsford Borough Council	13	www.chelmsford.gov.uk	01245 606 606
Cheltenham Borough Council	6	www.cheltenham.gov.uk	01242 262 626
Cherwell District Council	6	www.cherwell-dc.gov.uk	01295 252 535
Cheshire East Council	2	www.cheshireeast.gov.uk	0300 123 5500
Cheshire West and Chester Council	2	www.cheshirewestandchester.gov.uk	0300 123 8123
Chesterfield Borough Council	12	www.chesterfieldbc.gov.uk	01246 345 345
Chichester District Council	15	www.chichester.gov.uk	01243 785 166
Chiltern District Council	9	www.chiltern.gov.uk	01494 729 000
Chorley Borough Council	8	www.chorley.gov.uk	01257 515 151
Christchurch Borough Council	21	www.dorsetforyou.com	01202 495 000
City of London	16	www.cityoflondon.gov.uk/Corporation	020 7606 3030
Colchester Borough Council	13	www.colchester.gov.uk	01206 282 222
Conwy County Borough Council	20	www.conwy.gov.uk	01492 574 000
Copeland Borough Council	5	www.copelandbc.gov.uk	0845 054 8600
Corby Borough Council	9	www.corby.gov.uk	01536 464 000
Cornwall Council	14	www.cornwall.gov.uk	0300 1234 100
Cotswold District Council	6	www.cotswold.gov.uk	01285 623 000
Coventry City Council	3	www.coventry.gov.uk	024 7683 3333
Craven District Council	5	www.cravendc.gov.uk	01756 700 600
Crawley Borough Council	15	www.crawley.gov.uk	01293 438 000
Croydon London Borough Council	4	www.croydon.gov.uk	020 8726 6000
Dacorum Borough Council	16	www.dacorum.gov.uk	01442 228 000
Darlington Borough Council	5	www.darlington.gov.uk	01325 380 651
Dartford Borough Council	19	www.dartford.gov.uk	01322 343 434
Daventry District Council	9	www.daventrydc.gov.uk	01327 871 100
Denbighshire County Council	20	www.denbighshire.gov.uk	01824 706 555
Derby City Council	12	www.derby.gov.uk	01332 293 111
Derbyshire Dales District Council	12	www.derbyshiredales.gov.uk	01629 761 100
Doncaster Metropolitan Borough Council	11	www.doncaster.gov.uk	01302 734 444
Dover District Council	19	www.dover.gov.uk	01304 821 199
Dudley Metropolitan Borough Council	3	www.dudley.gov.uk	01384 812 345
Durham County Council	5	www.durham.gov.uk	0191 123 7070
Ealing London Borough Council	17	www.ealing.gov.uk	020 8825 5000
East Cambridgeshire District Council	13	www.eastcambs.gov.uk	01353 665 555
East Devon District Council	14	www.eastdevon.gov.uk	01395 516 551
East Dorset District Council	21	www.dorsetforyou.com	01202 886 201
East Hampshire District Council	15	www.easthants.gov.uk	01730 266 551
East Hertfordshire District Council	16	www.eastherts.gov.uk	01279 655 261
East Lindsey District Council	7	www.e-lindsey.gov.uk	01507 601 111
East Northamptonshire District Council	9	www.east-northamptonshire.gov.uk	01832 742 000
East Riding of Yorkshire Council	7	www.eastriding.gov.uk	01482 393 939
East Staffordshire Borough Council	1	www.eaststaffsbc.gov.uk	01283 508 000
Eastbourne Borough Council	15	www.eastbourne.gov.uk	01323 410 000
Eastleigh Borough Council	21	www.eastleigh.gov.uk	023 8068 8068
Eden District Council	5	www.eden.gov.uk	01768 817 817
Elmbridge Borough Council	5	www.elmbridge.gov.uk	01372 474 474
Enfield London Borough Council	17	www.enfield.gov.uk	020 8379 1000
Epping Forest District Council	13	www.eppingforestdc.gov.uk	01992 564 000
Epsom and Ewell Borough Council	5	www.epsom-ewell.gov.uk	01372 732 000
Erewash Borough Council	12	www.erewash.gov.uk	0115 907 2244
Exeter City Council	14	www.exeter.gov.uk	01392 277 888
Fareham Borough Council	21	www.fareham.gov.uk	01329 236 100
Fenland District Council	13	www.fenland.gov.uk	01354 654 321
Flintshire County Council	20	www.flintshire.gov.uk	01352 752 121
Forest Heath District Council	7	www.forest-heath.gov.uk	01638 719 000
Forest of Dean District Council	6	www.fdean.gov.uk	01594 810 000
Fylde Borough Council	8	www.fylde.gov.uk	01253 658 658
Gateshead Metropolitan Borough Council	5	www.gateshead.gov.uk	01914 333 000
Gedling Borough Council	11	www.gedling.gov.uk	01159 013 901
Gloucester City Council	6	www.gloucester.gov.uk	01452 522 232
Gosport Borough Council	21	www.gosport.gov.uk	023 9258 4242
Gravesham Borough Council	19	www.gravesham.gov.uk	01474 337 000
Great Yarmouth Borough Council	7	www.great-yarmouth.gov.uk	01493 856 100
Greenwich London Borough Council	18	www.greenwich.gov.uk	020 8854 8888

LOCAL LAND CHARGES SEARCHES & ENQUIRIES

Guildford Borough Council	5	www.guildford.gov.uk	01483 505 050
Gwynedd County Council	20	www.gwynedd.gov.uk	01286 672 255
Hackney London Borough Council	16	www.hackney.gov.uk	020 8356 3000
Halton Borough Council	2	www.halton.gov.uk	01519 078 300
Hambleton District Council	5	www.hambleton.gov.uk	08451 211 555
Hammersmith and Fulham London Borough Council	2	www.lbhf.gov.uk	020 8753 4040
Harborough District Council	9	www.harborough.gov.uk	01858 828 282
Haringey London Borough Council	17	www.haringey.gov.uk	020 8489 0000
Harlow District Council	13	www.harlow.gov.uk	01279 446 655
Harrogate Borough Council	5	www.harrogate.gov.uk	01423 500 600
Harrow London Borough Council	17	www.harrow.gov.uk	020 8863 5611
Hart District Council	21	www.hart.gov.uk	01252 622 122
Hartlepool Borough Council	5	www.hartlepool.gov.uk	01429 266 522
Hastings Borough Council	15	www.hastings.gov.uk	0845 274 1066
Havant Borough Council	15	www.havant.gov.uk	023 9247 4174
Havering London Borough Council	16	www.havering.gov.uk	01708 434 343
Hertsmere Borough Council	16	www.hertsmere.gov.uk	02082 072 277
High Peak Borough Council	12	www.highpeak.gov.uk	0845 129 7777
Hillingdon London Borough Council	17	www.hillingdon.gov.uk	01895 250 111
Hinckley and Bosworth Borough Council	9	www.hinckleyandbosworthonline.org.uk	01455 238 141
Horsham District Council	15	www.horsham.gov.uk	01403 215 100
Hounslow London Borough Council	17	www.hounslow.gov.uk	020 8583 2000
Huntingdonshire District Council	13	www.huntsdc.gov.uk	01480 388 388
Hyndburn Borough Council	8	www.hyndburnbc.gov.uk	01254 388 111
Ipswich Borough Council	7	www.ipswich.gov.uk	01473 432 000
Isle of Anglesey County Council	20	www.anglesey.gov.uk	01248 750 057
Council of the Isles of Scilly	14	www.scilly.gov.uk	01720 422 537
Isle of Wight Council	15	iwight.com	01983 821 000
Islington London Borough Council	16	www.islington.gov.uk	020 7527 2000
Kensington and Chelsea Royal Borough Council	2	www.rbkc.gov.uk	020 7361 3000
Kettering Borough Council	9	www.kettering.gov.uk	01536 410 333
King's Lynn and West Norfolk Borough Council	7	www.west-norfolk.gov.uk	01553 616 200
Kingston upon Hull City Council	7	www.hullcc.gov.uk	01482 300 300
Royal Borough of Kingston upon Thames	4	www.kingston.gov.uk	020 8547 5757
Kirklees Council	12	www.kirklees.gov.uk	01484 221 000
Knowsley Metropolitan Borough Council	1	www.knowsley.gov.uk	01514 896 000
Lambeth London Borough Council	18	www.lambeth.gov.uk	020 7926 1000
Lancaster City Council	8	www.lancaster.gov.uk	01524 582 000
Leeds City Council	12	www.leeds.gov.uk	01132 348 080
Leicester City Council	9	www.leicester.gov.uk	01162 527 000
Lewes District Council	15	www.lewes.gov.uk	01273 471 600
Lewisham London Borough Council	18	www.lewisham.gov.uk	020 8314 6000
Lichfield District Council	1	www.lichfielddc.gov.uk	01543 308 000
Lincoln City Council	7	www.lincoln.gov.uk	01522 881 188
Liverpool City Council	1	www.liverpool.gov.uk	0151 233 3000
Luton Borough Council	13	www.luton.gov.uk	01582 546 000
Maidstone Borough Council	19	www.maidstone.gov.uk	01622 602 000
Maldon District Council	13	www.maldon.gov.uk	01621 854 477
Malvern Hills District Council	3	www.malvernhills.gov.uk	01684 862 151
Manchester City Council	10	www.manchester.gov.uk	01612 345 000
Mansfield District Council	11	www.mansfield.gov.uk	01623 463 463
Medway Council	19	www.medway.gov.uk	01634 306 000
Melton Borough Council	9	www.melton.gov.uk	01664 502 502
Mendip District Council	21	www.mendip.gov.uk	01749 648 999
Merthyr Tydfil County Borough Council	20	www.merthyr.gov.uk	01685 725 000
Merton London Borough Council	4	www.merton.gov.uk	020 8274 4901
Mid Devon District Council	14	www.middevon.gov.uk	01884 255 255
Mid Suffolk District Council	7	www.midsuffolk.gov.uk	01449 720 711
Mid Sussex District Council	15	www.midsussex.gov.uk	01444 458 166
Middlesbrough Council	5	www.middlesbrough.gov.uk	01642 245 432
Milton Keynes Borough Council	9	www.miltonkeynes.gov.uk	01908 691 691
Mole Valley District Council	5	www.mole-valley.gov.uk	01306 885 001
Monmouthshire County Council	20	www.monmouthshire.gov.uk	01633 644 644
Neath Port Talbot County Borough Council	20	www.neath-porttalbot.gov.uk	01639 763 333
New Forest District Council	21	www.nfdc.gov.uk	023 8028 5000
Newark and Sherwood District Council	11	www.newark-sherwooddc.gov.uk	01636 650 000
Newcastle under Lyme Borough Council	1	www.newcastle-staffs.gov.uk	01782 717 717
Newcastle upon Tyne City Council	5	www.newcastle.gov.uk	01912 328 520
Newham London Borough Council	16	www.newham.gov.uk	020 8430 2000
Newport City Council	20	www.newport.gov.uk	01633 656 656
North Devon District Council	14	www.northdevon.gov.uk	01271 327 711
North Dorset District Council	21	www.north-dorset.gov.uk	01258 454 111
North East Derbyshire District Council	12	www.ne-derbyshire.gov.uk	01246 231 111
North East Lincolnshire Council	7	www.nelincs.gov.uk	01472 313 131
North Hertfordshire District Council	16	www.north-herts.gov.uk	01462 474 000
North Kesteven District Council	7	www.n-kesteven.gov.uk	01529 414 155
North Lincolnshire Council	7	www.northlincs.gov.uk/NorthLincs	01724 296 296
North Norfolk District Council	7	www.north-norfolk.gov.uk	01263 513 811

LOCAL LAND CHARGES SEARCHES & ENQUIRIES

Council		Website	Phone
North Somerset District Council	14	www.n-somerset.gov.uk	01934 888 888
North Tyneside Metropolitan Borough Council	5	www.northtyneside.gov.uk	01912 005 000
North Warwickshire Borough Council	6	www.northwarks.gov.uk	01827 715 341
North West Leicestershire District Council	9	www.nwleics.gov.uk	01530 454 545
Northampton Borough Council	9	www.northampton.gov.uk	01604 837 837
Northumberland County Council	5	www.northumberland.gov.uk	0845 600 6400
Norwich City Council	7	www.norwich.gov.uk	01603 212 212
Nottingham City Council	11	www.nottinghamcity.gov.uk	01159 155 555
Nuneaton and Bedworth Borough Council	6	www.nuneatonandbedworth.gov.uk	024 7637 6376
Oadby and Wigston Borough Council	9	www.oadby-wigston.gov.uk	01162 888 961
Oldham Metropolitan Borough Council	10	www.oldham.gov.uk	01619 113 000
Oxford City Council	6	www.oxford.gov.uk	01865 249 811
Pembrokeshire County Council	20	www.pembrokeshire.gov.uk	01437 764 551
Pendle Borough Council	8	www.pendle.gov.uk	01282 661 661
Peterborough City Council	13	www.peterborough.gov.uk	01733 747 474
Plymouth City Council	14	www.plymouth.gov.uk	01752 668 000
Borough of Poole	21	www.boroughofpoole.com	01202 633 633
Portsmouth City Council	15	www.portsmouth.gov.uk	023 9282 2251
Powys County Council	20	www.powys.gov.uk	01597 826 000
Preston City Council	8	www.preston.gov.uk	01772 906 000
Purbeck District Council	21	www.purbeck.gov.uk	01929 556 561
Reading Borough Council	6	www.reading.gov.uk	01189 390 900
Redbridge London Borough Council	16	www.redbridge.gov.uk	020 8554 5000
Redcar and Cleveland Borough Council	5	www.redcar-cleveland.gov.uk	0845 612 6126
Redditch Borough Council	3	www.redditchbc.gov.uk	0152 764 252
Reigate and Banstead Borough Council	5	www.reigate-banstead.gov.uk	01737 276 000
Rhondda Cynon Taff County Borough Council	20	www.rhondda-cynon-taff.gov.uk	01443 424000
Ribble Valley Borough Council	8	www.ribblevalley.gov.uk	01200 425 111
Richmond upon Thames London Borough Council	18	www.richmond.gov.uk	020 8891 1411
Richmondshire District Council	5	www.richmondshire.gov.uk	01748 829 100
Rochdale Metropolitan Borough Council	10	www.rochdale.gov.uk	01706 647 474
Rochford District Council	13	www.rochford.gov.uk	01702 546 366
Rossendale Borough Council	8	www.rossendale.gov.uk	01706 217 777
Rother District Council	15	www.rother.gov.uk	01424 787 878
Rotherham Metropolitan Borough Council	11	www.rotherham.gov.uk	01709 382 121
Rugby Borough Council	6	www.rugby.gov.uk	01788 533 533
Runnymede Borough Council	5	www.runnymede.gov.uk	01932 838 383
Rushcliffe Borough Council	11	www.rushcliffe.gov.uk	01159 819 911
Rushmoor Borough Council	21	www.rushmoor.gov.uk	01252 398 398
Rutland County Council	9	www.rutland.gov.uk	01572 722 577
Ryedale District Council	5	www.ryedale.gov.uk	01653 600 666
Salford City Council	11	www.salford.gov.uk	01617 459 529
Sandwell Metropolitan Borough Council	3	www.sandwell.gov.uk	01215 692 200
Scarborough Borough Council	5	www.scarborough.gov.uk	0800 371 695
Sedgemoor District Council	14	www.sedgemoor.gov.uk	0845 408 2540
Sefton Council	1	www.sefton.gov.uk	0845 140 0845
Selby District Council	5	www.selby.gov.uk	01757 705 101
Sevenoaks District Council	19	www.sevenoaks.gov.uk	01732 227 000
Sheffield City Council	11	www.sheffield.gov.uk	01142 726 444
Shepway District Council	19	www.shepway.gov.uk	01303 853 000
Shropshire Council	18	www.shropshire.gov.uk	0345 678 9000
Slough Borough Council	6	www.slough.gov.uk	01753 475 111
Solihull Metropolitan Borough Council	3	www.solihull.gov.uk	01217 046 000
South Bucks District Council	9	www.southbucks.gov.uk	01895 837 200
South Cambridgeshire District Council	13	www.scambs.gov.uk	08450 450 500
South Derbyshire District Council	12	www.south-derbys.gov.uk	01283 221 000
South Gloucestershire Council	6	www.southglos.gov.uk	01454 868 009
South Hams District Council	14	www.south-hams-dc.gov.uk	01803 861 234
South Holland District Council	7	www.sholland.gov.uk	01775 761 161
South Kesteven District Council	7	www.skdc.com	01476 406 080
South Lakeland District Council	5	www.southlakeland.gov.uk	01539 733 333
South Norfolk Council	7	www.south-norfolk.gov.uk	01508 533 633
South Northamptonshire Council	9	www.southnorthants.gov.uk	08452 300 226
South Oxfordshire District Council	6	www.southoxon.gov.uk	01491 823 000
South Ribble Borough Council	8	www.southribble.gov.uk	01772 421 491
South Somerset District Council	21	www.southsomerset.gov.uk	01935 462 462
South Staffordshire Council	1	www.sstaffs.gov.uk	01902 696 000
South Tyneside Metropolitan Borough Council	5	www.southtyneside.info	01914 277 000
Southampton City Council	21	www.southampton.gov.uk	023 8022 3855
Southend on Sea Borough Council	13	www.southend.gov.uk	01702 215 000
Southwark London Borough Council	18	www.southwark.gov.uk	020 7525 5000
Spelthorne Borough Council	5	www.spelthorne.gov.uk	01784 451 499
St Albans District Council	16	www.stalbans.gov.uk	01727 866 100
St Edmundsbury Borough Council	7	www.stedmundsbury.gov.uk	01284 763 233
St Helens Metropolitan Borough Council	1	www.sthelens.gov.uk	01744 456 789

LOCAL LAND CHARGES SEARCHES & ENQUIRIES

Council		Website	Phone
Stafford Borough Council	1	www.staffordbc.gov.uk	01785 619 000
Staffordshire Moorlands District Council	1	www.staffsmoorlands.gov.uk	01538 483 483
Stevenage Borough Council	16	www.stevenage.gov.uk	01438 242 242
Stockport Metropolitan Borough Council	10	www.stockport.gov.uk	01614 804 949
Stockton-on-Tees Borough Council	5	www.stockton.gov.uk	01642 393 939
Stoke on Trent City Council	1	www.stoke.gov.uk	01782 234 567
Stratford on Avon District Council	6	www.stratford.gov.uk	01789 267 575
Stroud District Council	6	www.stroud.gov.uk	01453 766 321
Suffolk Coastal District Council	7	www.suffolkcoastal.gov.uk	01394 383 789
Sunderland City Council	5	www.sunderland.gov.uk	01915 205 555
Surrey Heath Borough Council	5	www.surreyheath.gov.uk	01276 707 100
Sutton London Borough Council	4	www.sutton.gov.uk	020 8770 5000
Swale Borough Council	19	www.swale.gov.uk	01795 424 341
Swansea City and Borough Council	20	www.swansea.gov.uk	01792 636 000
Swindon Borough Council	21	www.swindon.gov.uk	01793 463 725
Tameside Metropolitan Borough Council	10	www.tameside.gov.uk	01613 428 355
Tamworth Borough Council	1	www.tamworth.gov.uk	01827 709 709
Tandridge District Council	5	www.tandridge.gov.uk	01883 722 000
Taunton Deane Borough Council	14	www.tauntondeane.gov.uk	01823 356 356
Teignbridge District Council	14	www.teignbridge.gov.uk	01626 361 101
Telford & Wrekin Council	18	www.telford.gov.uk	01952 380 000
Tendring District Council	13	www.tendringdc.gov.uk	01255 686 868
Test Valley Borough Council	21	www.testvalley.gov.uk	01264 368 000
Tewkesbury Borough Council	6	www.tewkesburybc.gov.uk	01684 295 010
Thanet District Council	19	www.thanet.gov.uk	01843 577 000
Three Rivers District Council	16	www.threerivers.gov.uk	01923 776 611
Thurrock Council	13	www.thurrock.gov.uk	01375 652 652
Tonbridge and Malling Borough Council	19	www.tmbc.gov.uk	01732 844 522
Torbay Council	14	www.torbay.gov.uk	01803 201 201
Torfaen County Borough Council	20	www.torfaen.gov.uk	01495 762 200
Torridge District Council	14	www.torridge.gov.uk	01237 428 700
Tower Hamlets London Borough Council	16	www.towerhamlets.gov.uk	020 7364 5000
Trafford Metropolitan Borough	10	www.trafford.gov.uk	01619 122 000
Tunbridge Wells Borough Council	19	www.tunbridgewells.gov.uk	01892 526 121
Uttlesford District Council	13	www.uttlesford.gov.uk	01799 510 510
Vale of Glamorgan Council	20	www.valeofglamorgan.gov.uk	01446 700 111
Vale of White Horse District Council	6	www.whitehorsedc.gov.uk	01235 520 202
City of Wakefield Metropolitan District Council	12	www.wakefield.gov.uk	01924 306 090
Walsall Metropolitan Borough Council	3	www.walsall.gov.uk	01922 650 000
Waltham Forest London Borough	16	www.lbwf.gov.uk	020 8496 3000
Wandsworth Borough Council	18	www.wandsworth.gov.uk	020 8871 6000
Warrington Borough Council	2	www.warrington.gov.uk	01925 444 400
Warwick District Council	6	www.warwickdc.gov.uk	01926 450 000
Watford Borough Council	16	www.watford.gov.uk	01923 226 400
Waveney District Council	7	www.waveney.gov.uk	01502 562 111
Waverley Borough Council	5	www.waverley.gov.uk	01483 523 333
Wealden District Council	15	www.wealden.gov.uk	01323 443 322
Wellingborough Borough Council	9	www.wellingborough.gov.uk	01933 229 777
Welwyn Hatfield District Council	16	www.welhat.gov.uk	01707 357 000
West Berkshire Council	6	www.westberks.gov.uk	01635 424 00
West Devon Borough Council	14	www.westdevon.gov.uk	01822 813 600
West Dorset District Council	21	www.dorsetforyou.com	01305 251 010
West Lancashire District Council	8	www.westlancsdc.gov.uk	01695 577 177
West Lindsey District Council	7	www.west-lindsey.gov.uk	01427 676 676
West Oxfordshire District Council	6	www.westoxon.gov.uk	01993 861 000
West Somerset District Council	14	www.westsomersetonline.gov.uk	01643 703 704
Westminster City Council	4	www.westminster.gov.uk	020 7641 6000
Weymouth and Portland Borough Council	21	www.weymouth.gov.uk	01305 838 000
Wigan Metropolitan Borough Council	10	www.wiganmbc.gov.uk	01942 244 991
Wiltshire Council	21	www.wiltshire.gov.uk	0300 456 0100
Winchester City Council	21	www.winchester.gov.uk	01962 840 222
Windsor and Maidenhead Royal Borough Council	6	www.rbwm.gov.uk	01628 798 888
Wirral Metropolitan Borough Council	1	www.wirral.gov.uk	01516 062 000
Woking Borough Council	5	www.woking.gov.uk	01483 755 855
Wokingham District Council	6	www.wokingham.gov.uk	01189 746 000
Wolverhampton City Council	3	www.wolverhampton.gov.uk	01902 551 155
Worcester City Council	3	www.cityofworcester.gov.uk	01905 723 471
Worthing Borough Council	15	www.worthing.gov.uk	01903 239 999
Wrexham County Borough Council	20	www.wrexham.gov.uk	01978 292 000
Wychavon District Council	3	www.wychavon.gov.uk	01386 565 000
Wycombe District Council	9	www.wycombe.gov.uk	01494 461 000
Wyre Borough Council	8	www.wyrebc.gov.uk	01253 891 000
Wyre Forest District Council	3	www.wyreforestdc.gov.uk	01562 732 928
York City Council	5	www.york.gov.uk	01904 613 161

4. DRAINAGE & WATER SEARCHES

It is recommended that a Con 29 DW drainage and water search is undertaken as part of every property purchase. Details of the Water Service Companies and their respective fees (as at the date of publication of this guide) are as follows:-

Company and water region   **Fee (inc. vat)**

Northumbrian Water – send Con 29 DW to:
Northumbrian Water
Property Solutions
PO Box 338
Durham DH1 5ZR
DX 717042 Durham 15
Tel: 0870 241 7408
Fax: 0870 241 7409
E-mail: propertysolutions@nwl.co.uk
Website: www.nwpropertysolutions.co.uk

£41.60 – residential search
£92.00 – commercial search

United Utilities – send Con 29 DW to:
United Utilities
Property Searches
Stephens Way
Goose Green
Wigan WN3 6PJ
DX 719690 Wigan 8
Tel: 0870 751 0101
Fax: 0870 751 0102
E-mail: property.searches@uuplc.co.uk
Website: www.unitedutilities.com

£41.81 – domestic search
£98.80 – commercial search

Yorkshire Water – send Con 29 DW to:
Safe-Move
P O Box 99
Bradford BD3 7YB
DX 723020 Bradford 20
Freephone: 0800 138 5385
Fax: 01274 804086
E-mail: safemove@yorkshirewater.com
Website: www.safe-move.co.uk

£41.40 – residential search
£105.75 – commercial search

Anglian Water – send Con 29 DW to:
Geodesys
Property Information Centre
P O Box 485
Huntingdon PE29 6YB
DX 123730 Huntingdon 6
Tel: 01480 323889
Fax: 01480 323890
E-mail: contactus@geodesys.com
Website: www.geodesys.com

£41.40 – standard search
£112.70 – commercial search

Severn Trent – send Con 29 DW to:
Severn Trent Searches
P O Box 6187

£46.00 – residential search
£75.00 (plus VAT) – commercial search (basic)

DRAINAGE & WATER SEARCHES

Nottingham NG5 1LE

DX 26205 Sherwood Rise

Tel: 0115 962 7269
Fax: 0115 962 7132
E-mail: searches@severntrent.co.uk
Website: www.severntrentsearches.com

£90.00 (plus VAT) – commercial search (standard)
£215.00 (plus VAT) – commercial search (extra)

Thames Water – send Con 29 DW to:
Thames Water Property Insight

£42.60 (ex VAT) – standard search
£98.00 (ex VAT) – commercial search

PO Box 3189
Slough SL1 4WW
DX 151280 Slough 13
Tel: 0118 925 1504
Fax: 0118 923 6655/57
E-mail: searches@thameswater.co.uk
Website: www.twpropertyinsight.co.uk

Southern Water – send Con 29 DW to:
Southern Water
Land Search Team
Southern House
Capstone Road
Chatham
Kent ME5 7QA
DX 400450 Chatham 5
Tel: 0845 270 0212
Fax: 01634 844514
Email: searches@southernwater.co.uk
Website: www.southernwater.co.uk/landsearches

£45.02 – residential search
£95.19 – commercial search

Wessex Water – send Con 29 DW to:
Wessex Water
Searches Team
Operations Centre
Claverton Down Road
Claverton Down
Bath BA2 7WW
DX 146200 Bath 6
Tel: 01225 526206
Fax: 01225 528923
E-mail: contactus@searches-online.com
Website: searches-online.com

£41.13 – residential search
£99.88 – commercial search

South West Water – send Con 29 DW to:
South West Water
Peninsula House
Rydon Lane
Exeter EX2 7HR
DX 119851 Exeter 10
Tel: 08453 303 401
Fax: 01392 442726
Website: www.southwestwater.co.uk/conveyancing

£46.58 – residential search
£104.65 – commercial search

Dwr Cymru Cyfyngedig (Welsh Water) – for Wales and English Border regions

send CON 29 DW to:
NDC Welsh Water
Po Box 10
Treharris CF46 6XZ
Tel: 01443 331155
Fax: 01443 331161
Website:
www.dwrcymrusearches.com
It is recommended that a telephone enquiry is made of Welsh Water if the property falls within part of the Dee Valley as a separate fee might then be payable for a Con 29 DW search.

£30.00 – standard search
£76.38 – expedited search

5. COMMONS REGISTRATION SEARCH

With effect from 1 August 2007, a commons search can only be made by raising enquiry 22 on form CON 29O Optional Enquiries of Local Authority.

6. ENVIRONMENTAL SEARCHES AND REPORTS

Information on contaminated land and environmental liabilities is available on the Law Society's website – www.lawsoc.org.uk.

The Environment Agency no longer supplies Property Search Reports. Instead it has a number of authorised resellers who offer a range of reports covering both residential and commercial property that contain all relevant Environment Agency data. These suppliers are:

GroundSure Limited
Tel: 01273 819500
Website: www.groundsure.com

Landmark Information Group
Tel: 0870 606 1700
Website: www.landmarkinfo.co.uk

7. COAL MINING SEARCHES AND REPORTS

The Law Society/Coal Authority scheme for coal mining enquiries was revised in October 2006. Form CON 29M (2006) has been extended to include enquiries covering brine subsidence claims. The Coal Mining and Brine Subsidence Claim Searches Directory and Guidance – 6th edition is available to be viewed/downloaded at www.coal.gov.uk/services/propertysearch/gazetteer/guidancenotesenglandandwales.cfm. It is also now possible to carry out a Ground Stability Search. Such a search will be relevant throughout England & Wales as natural ground instability can occur in anywhere.

A search can be ordered electronically, either through a National Land Information Service (NLIS) Channel Provider, through a private sector search company or directly using the Coal Authority's own on-line service. Searches can also be made by post, fax or telephone.

Four types of reports are available using the online service of the Coal Authority at www.coalminingreports.co.uk:
- Coal & Brine Residential property search
- Coal & Brine Non-residential property, commercial or site search
- Ground Stability Residential property search
- Ground Stability Non-residential property, commercial or site search

A postal search using form Con 29M (2006) (with a location plan showing the exact area of the search) should be sent to: –

The Coal Authority
Mining Reports Department
200 Lichfield Lane
Mansfield
NG18 4RG
DX 716176 Mansfield 5
Telephone requests : 0845 762 6848

Cheques should be made to the Coal Authority

Help Line: 01623 638203 (recorded information)
Fax: 01623 638338 (for urgent search requests when an *additional* "expedited fee" is payable – see the list below).
E-mail: mining reports@coal.gov.uk
Website and online service: www.coalminingreports.co.uk

The charges (inc VAT) are as follows.

A residential property search – postal or telephone users	£39.00
A residential property search – Coal Authority on-line service users	£31.05
A non-residential property or development site search – all users	£73.60
A "no search required" certificate (on-line service users only)	£14.95
Expedited Fee – payable additional to the above	£57.50
A residential ground stability report – Coal Authority on-line service users	£33.35 (off coalfield areas), £50.60 (on coalfield areas)
A residential ground stability report – postal or telephone users	£58.00
A non-residential, commercial or site ground stability report – Coal Authority on-line service users	£102.35
A non-residential, commercial or site ground stability report – postal or telephone users	£118.00

8. TIN AND COPPER MINING SEARCHES IN PARTS OF SOUTH WEST ENGLAND

Cornwall Consultants Limited can provide metalliferous (for example, tin and copper) mining search facilities for parts of Cornwall and Devon and can also carry out metalliferous mining searches for parts of Somerset and, in relation to stone mining searches for parts of northeast Somerset and West Wiltshire. The search is carried out by letter which must be accompanied by a plan and fee.

The address is:-

    Cornwall Consultants Limited
    Parc Vean House
    Coach Lane
    Redruth
    Cornwall TR15 2TT
    Tel: (01209) 313 511
    Fax: (01209) 313 512
    E-mail: mining@cornwallconsultants.co.uk
    Website: www.cornwallconsultants.co.uk

9. CHINA CLAY SEARCHES

Some properties in parts of Devon, Cornwall and Dorset might be affected by workings. The Kaolin and Ball Clay Association (UK) provides a postcode search service at www.kabca.org/postcode-search.php which allows an initial assessment of whether a property is in an area that may be affected by kaolin or ball clay development. If the Postcode Search reveals that a search is recommended it is necessary to submit an A4 plan showing the location of the property, together with the appropriate fee to obtain a specific report, as shown below. Incorrect cheques will be returned and the search deferred until the correct payment is received. There is no facility to undertake searches on-line.

For china clay searches in Cornwall and Devon:

    Imerys Minerals Ltd
    Par Moor Centre
    Par Moor Road
    Par
    Cornwall
    PL24 2SQ – marked for the attention of Adrian Mutton
    www.imerys.com
    Telephone: 01726 811311
    Fax: 01726 811200

For ball clay searches in Devon and Dorset:

    Sibelco UK Ltd
    Lovering Lodge
    Kingsteignton Road
    Newton Abbot
    Devon
    TQ12 2PA – marked for the attention of Clive Tompkins
    www.sibelco.co.uk
    Telephone: 01626 322331
    Fax: 01626 322388

The fee (as at the date of publication of this guide) is £56.00 plus VAT (£64.40) for a letter search and £70.00 plus VAT (£80.50) for a fax search, when an urgent reply is needed.

10. RADON SEARCHES

A Radon Risk Report can be obtained at www.ukradon.org. The fee is £3.45 per property. If the property does not have a postcode then a report can be obtained from Georeports (http://shop.bgs.ac.uk/georeports). The fee is £50.00.

Further details can be obtained from:

> Radon Survey
> Health Protection Agency
> Centre for Radiation, Chemical and Environmental Hazards
> Chilton
> Didcot
> OX11 0RQ
> Tel: 01235 822622
> Fax: 01235 833891
> E-mail: radon@hpa.org.uk
> Website: www.hpa.org.uk

> British Geological Survey
> Kingsley Dunham Centre
> Keyworth
> Nottingham
> NG12 5GG
> Tel: 0115 936 3143
> Fax: 0115 936 3276
> E-mail: enquiries@bgs.ac.uk
> Website: www.bgs.ac.uk

11. CHESHIRE BRINE SUBSIDENCE SEARCHES

The Cheshire Brine Search Report service is now operated by The Coal Authority and is incorporated in the CON 29M mining search, providing a combined coal and brine search report.

The fee is as follows:

CON29M Coal & Brine Residential Property Search
- Coal Authority On-Line Service Users £31.05
- Postal or Telephone Service Users £39.00

CON29M Coal & Brine Non-Residential Property or Site Search
- All Users £50 inc VAT

No Search Required Certificate
- (On-Line Service Users only) £73.60 inc VAT

Expedited Fee
- payable additional to the above £57.50 inc VAT

A search can be ordered electronically, either through a National Land Information Service (NLIS) Channel Provider, through a private sector search company or directly using the Coal Authority's own on-line service. Searches can also be made by post, fax or telephone.

When ordering by post, a cheque for the required amount (made payable to The Coal Authority) should be sent together with a CON29M search form and plan of the property to:

> The Coal Authority,
> Mining Reports,
> 200 Lichfield Lane,
> Mansfield,
> Nottinghamshire
> NG18 4RG
> DX 716176 MANSFIELD 5
> Telephone requests: 0845 762 6848
> Website and online service: www.coalminingreports.co.uk

12. COMPANIES HOUSE

Details of the various charges for postal and online enquiries are listed on the Companies House website – www.companieshouse.gov.uk.

The following are some examples of the prices for information available (as at the date of publication of this guide) from:

The Companies House Contact Centre

Tel: 0870 33 33 636 between 08:30 – 18:00 Monday to Friday, except national holidays

E-mail: enquiries@companies-house.gov.uk:

- **Companies**

Incorporation	£20.00
Electronic incorporation	£15.00
Same-day incorporation	£50.00
Same-day electronic incorporation	£30.00
Change of name	£10.00
Same-day change of name	£50.00
Same-day simultaneous re-registration and change of name	£100.00
Re-registration	£20.00
Same-day re-registration	£50.00
Annual document processing fee payable with annual return:	
Sent on paper	£30.00
Sent electronically	£15.00
Voluntary dissolution	£10.00
Registration of a charge per entry	£13.00

- **Oversea Companies**

Registration of a place of business or a branch of an oversea company	£20.00
Change of corporate name of an oversea company	£10.00
Annual document processing fee payable with oversea company accounts	£30.00
Same-day registration	£50.00

- **Limited Liability Partnerships (LLPs)**

Registration of LLP	£20.00
Same-day registration	£50.00
LLP annual document processing fee payable with annual return	£30.00
LLP change of name	£10.00
Same-day change of name	£50.00
LLP voluntary dissolution	£10.00
Registration of charge per entry by a LLP	£13.00

- **Limited Partnerships (LPs)**

Registration of a Limited Partnership	£2.00
Registration of statements of change	no charge

COMPANIES HOUSE

- **Companies House WebCHeck** (credit/debit card purchases only)
Download document images
Latest Accounts	£1.00
Latest Annual Return	£1.00
Latest Account & Annual Return	£2.00

Company Reports
The Company Record	£1.00
The Current Appointments Report	£1.00

- **Companies House Direct**
Sign on no charge
Monthly subscription (per account per month)	£5.00

Screen Charges
Company indexes no charge
Basic company details no charge
History of company transactions no charge
Register of Disqualified Directors no charge
Insolvency details no charge
Company appointments	£1.00
Personal appointments	£1.00

Company charge index no charge
Charge details	£1.00

Company Reports
The Current Appointments Report	£1.00
The Mortgage Statement	£1.00
The Company Record	£1.00

Document Images
Download per document	£1.00
On-line viewing per document	£4.00

Documents for post or fax
Per document by post	£3.00
By fax	£3.00

Mortgage Register as paper document

Document Packages (up to 50 documents)
by image download	£4.00
by post	£20.00

Monitor Service
Monitor request (per company, for 12 months)	£0.50
Monitor renewal (per company, for 12 months)	£0.50

Certified Copy Documents
Same day post/collection	£50.00
Ordinary service post/collection	£15.00

Certificates
Same day post/collection with fax copy (plus £3.00)	£50.00
Ordinary service post/collection with additional copy (plus £10.00)	£15.00

- **Information Centres**

Screen Charges
Company indexes no charge
Basic company details no charge
History of company transactions no charge
Register of Disqualified Directors no charge
Insolvency details no charge
Company appointments	£1.00
Personal appointments	£1.00

Company charge (incl. mortgage) index no charge
Charge details	£1.00

Company Reports
The Current Appointments Report	£1.00
The Mortgage Statement	£1.00
The Company Record	£1.00

Document Packages
Print (up to 25 documents)	£7.00

COMPANIES HOUSE

Document Orders

View document image	£2.00
Print document (without viewing)	£1.00
Inspection of information on hard file	£6.00
Paper copy of hard file document (per document)	£9.00
Online print of document or customer photocopies from microfiche per page	£0.10

Microfiche

Archive microfiche (copy of documents received up to 31.12.2002)	£9.00
Microfiche copy of a bulk shareholders list collected from Information Centre	£12.50

- **Contact Centre: 0870 33 33 636**

Screen Charges

Registered office address (per company) by telephone no charge

Screen Prints (per page)

Alphabetical index, dissolved companies, former names

By post	£2.00
By fax or email	£2.00

History screen and registered office (per company)
By post no charge
By fax or email no charge

Directors Register (company based enquiry)

By post	£3.00
By fax or email	£3.00

Charge (incl. mortgage) details each company

By post	£3.00
By fax or email	£3.00

Company Reports

By post

The Current Appointments Report	£3.00
The Mortgage Statement	£3.00
The Company Record	£3.00

By fax or email

The Current Appointments Report	£3.00
The Mortgage Statement	£3.00
The Company Record	£3.00

Document Images

By email (post – 1995 documents)

Copy of a company document	£3.00

Company Documents by post or fax

Paper copy of a company document	£3.00
Fax copy of a company document	£3.00
Paper copy of a document not on microfiche	£9.00

Paper copy of Charges (Incl. Mortgage) Register

By post	£3.00
By fax	£3.00
Paper copy of a bulk shareholder list (from fiche) max 20 pages £12.50 per page thereafter	£0.20

Microfiche

Archive microfiche (copy of documents received up to 31.12.02)	£9.00
Microfiche copy of a bulk shareholders list	£12.50

Addresses for postal enquiries:

Main Office	London Office
Companies House	Companies House
Crown Way	21 Bloomsbury Street
Maindy	London
Cardiff	WC1B 3XD
CF14 3UZ	
DX 33050 Cardiff	

13. GYPSUM MINING

British Gypsum Limited can supply information about the following areas:
- East Sussex;
- North Leicestershire;
- South Nottinghamshire;
- East Staffordshire;
- the southern part of North Yorkshire; and
- the eastern part of Cumbria.

Contact:

Mr C Thomas – The Company Surveyor
British Gypsum Limited
Geological and Mining Services
East Leake Works
Loughborough LE12 6JQ
Tel: 0115 945 1000

A location plan is always required. A fee is payable.

14. LAND REGISTRY DIRECT

This service enables its subscribers the facility of on-line access to registers of title and electronic delivery of applications for a range of other Land Registry services.

On-line results are available for Land Registry searches of whole (with priority) and for Land Charges searches against private individuals and companies.

Land Registry Direct is available (to subscribers to the service) between 07.00 to 22.00 Monday to Friday (excluding Bank Holidays). Saturday access is available to subscribers between 07.00 to 17.00, although some applications will be held and dealt with on the next working day.

For information about joining the service please contact:

Land Registry e-Services Team
Touthill Close
City Road
Peterborough
PE1 1XN
DX 12598 Peterborough
Tel 0870 0100299
E-mail: admin@landregistrydirect.gov.uk
Website: www.landregistrydirect.gov.uk

The following are examples of fees payable by subscribers to Land Registry Direct:

Fees for Land Registration Services using Land Registry Direct: –

Register View	£4.00
Title Plan View	£4.00
Document View	£6.00
Official Copy – title known:-	
– Electronic delivery of a copy of the register	£4.00
– Electronic delivery of a copy of the title plan	£4.00

– Electronic delivery of a copy of any or all documents referred to in the register (excluding a lease)	£6.00
– Electronic delivery of a copy of a lease	£12.00
– Postal delivery of a copy of the register	£8.00
– Postal delivery of a copy of the title plan	£8.00
– Postal delivery of a certificate of inspection of the title plan	£8.00
– Postal delivery of a copy of any or all documents referred to in the register (excluding a lease)	£12.00
– Postal delivery of a copy of a lease	£24.00
Official Copy when the title number is unknown	See * below
Official Search of Whole and Home Rights Search	£4.00
Day List Enquiry	No fee
Changes to the register	No fee
Search of the Index Map	See * below
Electronic Notification of Discharge	No fee

* At that date of publication of this guide there is a fee of £5.00 where the search discloses no registered titles or up to 5 registered titles. If the search reveals more than 5 titles, there is a fee of £5.00 for the first 5 titles and a further fee of £3.00 for each batch of up to 10 additional titles disclosed.

Fees for Land Charges Services using Land Registry Direct:

Full Search (private individual or limited company)	£2.00 per name
Bankruptcy Search (private individual)	£2.00 per name
Land Charges Registration View	£1.00 per name

Fees for Land Charges Services using Land Registry Direct (postal results)

Full Search Application (local authority or complex name)	£2.00 per name
Bankruptcy Search Application (complex name)	£2.00 per name
Office Copy Application	£1.00 per copy

15. THE NATIONAL LAND INFORMATION SERVICE ("NLIS")

The National Land Information Service ("NLIS") enables property searches to be made electronically, by contacting one of the NLIS licensed channel operators (see below) via the Internet.

NLIS therefore provides a single point of access, via each of the websites (set out below) to the usual sources of property information. Each of the websites lists the types of search that can be made.

Examples of the searches and enquiries that can be made in this way include:
- Local Authority
- Land Registry
- Water utilities
- Coal Authority
- Environment Agency
- Forestry Commission
- Highways Agency
- Electricity

INFORMATION AVAILABLE

- Gas
- Telecommunications
- London Transport
- Civil Aviation Authority
- British Waterways
- Ordnance Survey
- Speciality searches (e.g. radon, clay, tin mining, limestone, gypsum, Cheshire Brine, Cornish Tin, Chancel Repairs)
- Company searches

The NLIS system enables the land that is the subject of the search to be identified using the on-line Ordnance Survey digital mapping service, in conjunction with the National Land and Property Gazetteer. The Gazetteer allocates a "Unique Property Reference Number – UPRN" to enable each information provider to identify the subject land when that provider is contacted electronically (via one of the three channel service operators set out below).

A user must therefore know the usual address and postcode details for the subject property to be searched.

The relevant fees (that each of the channel operators charges for each type of search or enquiry) are listed on each of the channel service operators websites:
- Searchflow (www.searchflow.co.uk)
- TM Search (www.tmsearch.co.uk)

16. INFORMATION AVAILABLE FROM "ENGLISH HERITAGE"

The National Monument Record ("NMR") archives at English Heritage include:
- Survey records created over 90 years by the Royal Commission on the Historical Monuments of England.
- The collections of the National Buildings Record, created in 1941 to record the architectural heritage threatened by war, and now containing photographs of buildings in every parish in England.
- A major library of aerial photography, containing both vertical and oblique photography for the whole of England and including important historic coverage from the RAF, the Ordnance Survey and commercial sources.
- Collections of photographs, plans and other records acquired by the NMR from individuals, companies, government departments and other institutions.

The above types of information can sometimes be useful evidence in boundary dispute and adverse possession cases. Full details of the requirements of the service and the various fees that are payable are available from:

Enquiry and Research Services
National Monuments Record
English Heritage
Kemble Drive
Swindon SN2 2GZ
Tel: (01793) 414600
Fax: (01793) 414606
E-mail: nmrinfo@english-heritage.org.uk
Website: www.english-heritage.org.uk

17. LONDON UNDERGROUND SEARCHES

Where land is near London underground lines, enquiries about railway rights/liabilities and new works can be sent to:-

Railway Searches
Operational Property Division
TFL Group Property & Facilities
4th Floor
Victoria Station House
191 Victoria Street
London SW1E 5NE
Tel: 020 7918 3778
Fax: 020 7976 6563

An application should include:
- The full property address including postcode
- A copy of the Land Registry Title plan or an Ordnance Survey Plan extract (at 1:1250 scale) identifying the property
- A cheque for the fee, as appropriate, made payable to 'Transport for London'

The fees are:-
Residential property: £138.00
Commercial/development property: £207.00

Docklands Light Railway search requests should be sent to:

Serco Docklands Ltd
Castor Lane
London E14 0DS
Tel: 020 7363 9700

18. ORDNANCE SURVEY INFORMATION

Information about the various Ordnance Survey services that can assist conveyancers (with details of the fees payable) is available from: –

Ordnance Survey
Customer Service Centre
Romsey Road
Southampton
SO16 4GU
Tel: 0845 605 0505
Fax: 023 8079 2615
Email: customerservices@ordnancesurvey.co.uk
Website: www.ordnancesurvey.gov.uk

On-line applications for OS copyright licences can also be made on the above website.

19. CHANCEL REPAIR

The liability (described as a "right in respect of the repair of a church chancel") rarely appears on title deeds and does not depend on notice. See the decision of the House of Lords in *Aston Cantlow and Wilmcote with Billesley Parochial Church*

Council v Wallbank [2003] 3 All ER 1213. It was included as an "overriding interest" under the Land Registration Act 1925 (section 70(1)(c)).

The liability now falls within Schedules 1 and 3 to the Land Registration Act 2002 (see the Land Registration Act 2002 (Transitional Provisions) (No. 2) Order 2003). It will accordingly still have effect as an overriding interest, for the period of 10 years from 13 October 2003.

See also paragraph (15) of the list of applications for which no fee is payable (Schedule 4 to the Land Registration Fee Order 2009) as reproduced in Part 2.4 of this guide.

It is accordingly still important to identify whether a specific property is affected by the liability. Such identification is generally a matter of local knowledge or enquiry.

A leaflet – *"Chancel Repairs"* – can be obtained from:-

The National Archives
Ruskin Avenue
Kew
Near Richmond
Surrey TW9 4DU
Tel: 020 8876 3444
Website: www.nationalarchives.gov.uk.

ChancelCheck is an accurate screening report which will reveal whether or not a property is located within an historical parish where there continues to be a potential for chancel repair liability. The cost of a search is £17.63 and is available from:

Conveyancing Liability Solutions Limited
Suite 39
40 Churchill Square
Kings Hill
West Malling
Kent
ME19 4YU
Tel: 0870 013 0872
Fax: 0870 013 0190
E-mail: sales@clsl.co.uk
Website: www.clsl.co.uk

20. RATES OF INTEREST UNDER s 32 LAND COMPENSATION ACT 1961

1 July 1996	5.25%
31 December 1996	5.50%
30 June 1997	6.00%
30 September 1997	6.50%
31 December 1997	6.75%
30 June 1998	7.00%
31 December 1998	5.75%
31 March 1999	5.00%
30 June 1999	4.5%
30 September 1999	4.75%
4 January 2000	5.00%
31 March 2000	5.5%
2 April 2001	5.25%

2 July 2001	4.75%
1 October 2001	4.25%
31 December 2001	3.50%
31 March 2003	3.25%
30 September 2003	3.00%
31 December 2003	3.25%
31 March 2004	3.50%
30 June 2004	4.00%
30 September 2004	4.25%
30 September 2005	4.00%
2 October 2006	4.25%
2 January 2007	4.5%
2 April 2007	4.75%
2 July 2007	5.0%
1 October 2007	5.25%
31 December 2007	5.00%
31 March 2008	4.75%
30 June 2008	4.50%
31 December 2008	1.50%
31 March 2009	0.00%

21. LAW SOCIETY INTEREST RATES

The Law Society rate is 4% above Barclays Bank base rate. The following changes have taken place since January 1996:

18 January 1996	10.25%
8 March 1996	10%
6 June 1996	9.75%
30 October 1996	10%
6 May 1997	10.25%
6 June 1997	10.50%
10 July 1997	10.75%
7 August 1997	11%
6 November 1997	11.25%
4 June 1998	11.50%
8 October 1998	11.25%
5 November 1998	10.75%
10 December 1998	10.25%
7 January 1999	10%
4 February 1999	9.5%
8 April 1999	9.25%
10 June 1999	9%
8 September 1999	9.25%
4 November 1999	9.50%
13 January 2000	9.75%
10 February 2000	10%
8 February 2001	9.75%
5 April 2001	9.50%
10 May 2001	9.25%
2 August 2001	9%
18 September 2001	8.75%
4 October 2001	8.50%
8 November 2001	8%
6 February 2003	7.75%
10 July 2003	7.50%
6 November 2003	7.75%
5 February 2004	8%
6 May 2004	8.25%
10 June 2004	8.50%
5 August 2004	8.75%
4 August 2005	8.50%
3 August 2006	8.75%
9 November 2006	9%

11 January 2007 .... 9.25%
10 May 2007 .... 9.5%
5 July 2007 .... 9.75%
6 December 2007 .... 9.50%
7 February 2008 .... 9.25%
10 April 2008 .... 9.00%
8 October 2008 .... 8.5%
6 November 2008 .... 7%
4 December 2008 .... 6%
8 January 2009 .... 5.5%
5 February 2009 .... 5%
5 March 2009 .... 4.5%

22. OTHER TELEPHONE NUMBERS

County Councils:

Buckinghamshire County Council	www.buckscc.gov.uk	0845 370 8090
Cambridgeshire County Council	www.cambridgeshire.gov.uk	01223 717 111
Cumbria County Council	www.cumbriacc.gov.uk	01228 606 060
Derbyshire County Council	www.derbyshire.gov.uk	08456 058 058
Devon County Council	www.devon.gov.uk	01392 382 000
Dorset County Council	www.dorsetforyou.com	01305 251 000
East Sussex County Council	www.eastsussex.gov.uk	01273 481 000
Essex County Council	www.essexcc.gov.uk	08457 430 430
Gloucestershire County Council	www.gloucestershire.gov.uk	01452 425 000
Hampshire County Council	www.hants.gov.uk	01962 870 500
Herefordshire County Council	www.herefordshire.gov.uk	01432 260000
Hertfordshire County Council	www.hertsdirect.org	01438 737 599
Kent County Council	www.kent.gov.uk	08458 247 247
Lancashire County Council	www.lancashire.gov.uk	08450 530 000
Leicestershire County Council	www.leicestershire.gov.uk	01162 323 232
Lincolnshire County Council	www.lincolnshire.gov.uk	01522 782 060
Norfolk County Council	www.norfolk.gov.uk	0844 800 8020
North Yorkshire County Council	www.northyorks.gov.uk	01609 780 780
Northamptonshire County Council	www.northamptonshire.gov.uk	01604 236 236
Oxfordshire County Council	www.oxfordshire.gov.uk	01865 792 422
Rutland County Council	www.rutland.gov.uk	01572 722 577
Somerset County Council	www.somerset.gov.uk	0845 345 9166
Staffordshire County Council	www.staffordshire.gov.uk	01785 223 121
Suffolk County Council	www.suffolkcc.gov.uk	0845 606 6067
Surrey County Council	www.surreycc.gov.uk	08456 009 009
Warwickshire County Council	www.warwickshire.gov.uk	0845 090 7000
West Sussex County Council	www.westsussex.gov.uk	01243 777 100
Worcestershire County Council	www.worcestershire.gov.uk	01905 763 763

Greater London Authority — www.london.gov.uk — 020 7983 4000

National Park Authorities:

Brecon Beacons National Park Authority	www.breconbeacons.org	01874 624437
Broads Authority	www.broads-authority.gov.uk	01603 610734
Cairngorms National Park Authority	www.cairngorms.co.uk	01479 873535
Dartmoor National Park Authority	www.dartmoor-npa.gov.uk	01626 832093
Exmoor National Park Authority	www.exmoor-nationalpark.gov.uk	01398 323665
Lake District National Park Authority	www.lake-district.gov.uk	01539 724555
New Forest National Park Authority	www.newforestnpa.gov.uk	01590 646600
North York Moors National Park	www.visitnorthyorkshiremoors.co.uk	01439 770657
Northumberland National Park Authority	www.northumberlandnational-park.org.uk	01434 605555
Peak District National Park Authority	www.peakdistrict.gov.uk	01629 816200
Pembrokeshire Coast National Park Authority	www.pcnpa.org.uk	0845 345 7275
Snowdonia National Park Authority	www.snowdonia-npa.gov.uk	01766 770274
South Downs Joint Committee	www.southdowns.gov.uk	01243 558700
Yorkshire Dales National Park Authority	www.yorkshiredales.org.uk	0870 1 666333

Regional Development Agencies:

Advantage West Midlands	www.advantagewm.co.uk	0121 380 3500
East Midlands Development Agency	www.emda.org.uk	0115 988 8300
East of England Development Agency	www.eeda.org.uk	01223 713900
London Development Agency	www.lda.gov.uk	020 7593 8000
Northwest Regional Development Agency	www.nwda.co.uk	01925 400100
One NorthEast	www.onenortheast.co.uk	0191 229 6200
South East England Development Agency	www.seeda.co.uk	01483 484200
South West of England Regional Development Agency	www.southwestrda.org.uk	01392 214 747
Yorkshire Forward	www.yorkshire-forward.com	0113 3949600

Other useful telephone numbers:

Boundary Commission for England	www.statistics.gov.uk	020 7533 5177
British Waterways Board	www.britishwaterways.co.uk	01923 201 120

OTHER TELEPHONE NUMBERS

Department for Business, Enterprise and Regulatory Reform	www.berr.gov.uk	020 7215 5000
Communities and Local Government	www.communities.gov.uk	020 7944 4400
Natural England	www.naturalengland.org.uk	0845 600 3078
Crown Estate	www.thecrownestate.co.uk	020 7851 5000
Department for Environment, Food and Rural Affairs (Defra)	www.defra.gov.uk	0845 933 5577
Department for Transport	www.dft.gov.uk	020 7944 8300
Environment Agency	www.environment-agency.gov.uk	08708 506 506
Forestry Commission	www.forestry.gov.uk	0131 334 0303
Highways Agency	www.highways.gov.uk	08457 50 40 30
National Assembly for Wales	www.wales.gov.uk	029 20 825111
Planning Inspectorate	www.planning-inspectorate.gov.uk	0117 372 8000
Residential Property Tribunal Service	www.rpts.gov.uk	020 7446 7700
Valuation Office Agency	www.voa.gov.uk	020 7506 1700
The National Trust	www.nationaltrust.org.uk/main	0870 458 4000
Network Rail	www.networkrail.co.uk	020 7557 8000
The Royal Institution of Chartered Surveyors	www.rics.org	0870 333 1600
The National Housebuilding Council	www.nhbc.co.uk	01494 434477